Organising

Karen Gilchrist

Croner Publications Ltd
Croner House
London Road
Kingston upon Thames
Surrey KT2 6SR
Telephone: 0181-547 3333

Copyright © 1998 Croner Publications Ltd

Published by
Croner Publications Ltd
Croner House
London Road
Kingston upon Thames
Surrey KT2 6SR
Telephone: 0181-547 3333

All rights reserved. No part of this publication may be reproduced, stored in a retrieval system, or transmitted in any form or by any means, electronic, mechanical, photocopying, recording or otherwise, without the prior permission of Croner Publications Ltd.

While every care has been taken in the writing and editing of this book, readers should be aware that only Acts of Parliament and Statutory Instruments have the force of law, and that only the Courts can authoritatively interpret the law.

British Library Cataloguing-in-Publication Data. A catalogue record for this book is available from the British Library.

ISBN 1 85524 463 2

Phototypeset by Intype London Ltd
Printed by Whitstable Litho Printers Ltd, Whitstable, Kent

THE AUTHOR

KAREN GILCHRIST is a researcher and writer for communications company Resource Base. Her organisation produces a range of products for the education and voluntary sectors, including print, video and Web materials. In addition, Resource Base produces broadcast programmes on educational and social awareness issues. The company also organises training days for charities on media relations, communications and fundraising.

Before joining Resource Base, Karen worked for the media charity Community Service Volunteers, the ITV company Television South and television production company Workhouse. Karen trained as a magazine journalist with Centaur Communications after winning the annual Jenny Manton journalism prize.

THE REVIEWER

RUTH JONES is director of the independent youth arts development agency Artswork. Artswork develops and manages youth arts projects and training initiatives and works in partnership with youth and arts organisations, artists, local authorities, regional arts boards and young people. Artswork has specialist experience in working in the arts and young people at risk through its national initiative "Creating Futures".

Ruth has worked in youth and community arts for 10 years, and has organised a whole range of events including performances, conferences, press launches, exhibitions, festivals, workshops, training, and fundraising events. Before joining Artswork in 1995, she worked for a range of organisations including the Arts Council, local authority youth and community services and health promotion, a crafts gallery, and as a music workshop tutor.

CONTENTS

General Principles and Issues	1
Attention to detail, leave nothing to chance	1
Planning and preparation	2
Your event plan	4
Learning from others	21
Venue hire and liaison	22
Equality of access	27
Sponsorship	38
Documentation and correspondence	40
Legal issues and insurance	41
Audio visual and set	43
Petty cash	48
Childcare	49
Travel, transport and overnight accommodation	49
Event literature	51
The weather, heating and air conditioning	52
Prizes and merchandise	54
Refreshments and special diets	55
Getting people to the event	57
Briefings	60
Signposting	61
Car parking	63
Toilets	63
First aid	64
Registration/badging	65
What to wear	66
On-the-day communications	66
Checklists	67
Evaluation	70

Organising Effective Events

Specific Events

Annual general meetings	71
Auctions	73
Balls, dinners and themed evenings	74
Conferences	77
Exhibitions, roadshows and displays	80
Fairs and fêtes	82
Festivals	84
Fundraising special events	85
Open days	87
Openings and launches	89
Protests, demonstrations and vigils	90
Press conferences and photo opportunities	92
Seminars, workshops and training days	95

And Finally, ... 97

INTRODUCTION

There's no doubt that organising successful and effective events is hard work. No matter how many you have already organised you always have to put in a huge amount of time and effort to ensure an event is successful. However, the really important ingredients are careful planning and clear thinking. That's what this book is all about — helping you to plan and consider all eventualities.

The first part, "General Principles and Issues", runs through some of the basic rules of good event organisation. Whether you are setting up a small training workshop or planning a fundraising spectacular many of the same general principles and issues apply.

The second, and main, section of the book "Specific Events" looks at some of the principal types of events, highlighting particular tricks and traps to be aware of.

GENERAL PRINCIPLES AND ISSUES

ATTENTION TO DETAIL, LEAVE NOTHING TO CHANCE

"Attention to the minutest of details is vital. It's too easy to overlook something that will spoil the day or make things difficult," says Ruth Jones, director of Artswork. Ruth has organised a number of conferences, training courses, youth arts festivals, events, exhibitions, press launches and performances.

Every successful event organiser's slogan should be: "Attention to detail, leave nothing to chance". If you really apply this motto, then you will find that:

(a) the overall quality of the event will be raised and people's enjoyment will be greater. They might not attribute this to the chocolate biscuits and flower arrangements, but it all adds to the overall atmosphere of a successful event
(b) you will find the event itself less stressful and more rewarding
(c) you won't prevent things from going wrong, but you'll be ready to deal with any problems and have solutions ready to hand.

Organising Effective Events

PLANNING AND PREPARATION

"The essence of good event organisation is to allow plenty of time to organise the event, to be organised and prepared for every eventuality," says Charlotte Macpherson of the National Council for Voluntary Organisations. She organises their annual conference and exhibition stands.

Planning and preparation are absolutely essential to successful event organisation. While thinking and talking about the event are important, writing things down is crucial. You can keep checking back on progress and you can circulate the paper so that other people know what is going on. If you want to attract sponsorship it will also give you a good basis for your proposal.

A good event plan will include the following:

- aims and objectives: summarising why you are organising the event and what you hope to achieve (that way you'll be able to evaluate whether or not you've been successful)
- the target audience: so you know who you want to attract to the event
- the event format: clarifying the structure and components
- the date: when are you going to hold the event?
- branding and themes: what the event is all about
- budget and pricing: taking account of all the time you will spend on organising, as well as direct costs
- responsibilities/lines of command: explaining which elements can be delegated and who has ultimate responsibility
- response mechanisms and administrative support: ensuring you have adequate support
- marketing and promotion: setting out your strategy to ensure people know about the event and attend
- timetables: outlining target dates and absolute deadlines
- on the day staffing: ensuring people book the date in their diaries in plenty of time.

All of these elements are set out in more detail below. First, there are some other points to make about planning and preparation.

1. Brainstorm with others. Planning is much easier if you work with other members of your organisation, or others who are going to be involved in the event. Involving others from the outset is important if you don't want to end up doing all the work. If people have helped to develop the event idea then they will be more committed to its success. They will also be clearer about their own role.
2. Events evolve. You might end up with an event that doesn't look like the one described in your original plan. This isn't a problem as long as you are clear about why changes have been made and that they are changes for the better. It's also obviously important to re-work both your timetable and budget as things alter.
3. Invest time in planning. You might think that as time is limited, why waste it writing things down. If you put time and energy into planning from the start, you will save yourself lots of time and worry later on. Even if you are the only one to refer to your written notes it's still worth doing, for the following reasons:

    - you can reassure yourself with the realistic timetable that everything will get done in time, when it seems there are still hundreds of things to sort out. Alternatively you can assess whether or not you need extra support and put a strong case together for funders or managers
    - you can motivate yourself by going back to why you're running the event and what you're hoping to achieve
    - you can adapt the plan for future events, and save re-inventing the wheel.

YOUR EVENT PLAN

AIMS AND OBJECTIVES, WHY?

You probably already have a broad idea as to why you are organising your event. But it's worth teasing this out a bit and setting out aims and objectives. This is where colleagues and funders can also feed in some valuable thoughts.

It's worth knowing, for instance, what a funder wants to achieve. Usually this will be different, but complementary, to your own aims. If they weren't in sympathy with your aims then they wouldn't be funding the event.

Your overall objective/s will be one or more broad statements relating to such issues as:

- awareness raising ("to raise awareness of our charity/our campaign", "to discuss and debate the issues relating to...")
- education and training ("to increase delegates' skills and knowledge in the areas of...") fundraising targets ("to raise £... for our charity", "to attract new sponsorship for ...")
- entertainment ("to bring the local community together through a performance of...")
- sharing information ("to inform supporters, volunteers and staff of projects and achievements throughout the year", "to brief staff on forthcoming campaigns and events")
- motivation and reward ("to celebrate the achievements of..., to inspire others and to motivate them to continue").

Your specific aims will cover a whole range of issues, either directly or indirectly relating to the event. They could relate to:

- the audience ("to attract 100 key opinion formers from local government...", "to ensure the event is accessible to all potential delegates...")

General Principles and Issues

- the tone of the event ("to run a high quality, prestigious and memorable event", "to ensure delegates are comfortable and able to network easily...")
- the sponsor's role ("to show that ... is actively involved in the local community")
- the outcomes ("to produce a report summarising the views of participants", "to develop an action plan for the local community...")
- publicity ("to secure press and radio coverage in advance of the event", "to attract local media to the event").

These are just examples to suggest how you might set out your aims and objectives as punchy bullet points that are easy to refer to and will make sense to everyone involved in the event. They will be particularly helpful when you come to evaluate the success of the event.

TARGET AUDIENCE

Another important element in your planning is the target audience. If you don't know who you hope to attract to your event then you won't be able to work out your promotional and pricing policies.

"Even if your target audience is 'everyone' you should define who that everyone is — you may have missed someone," says Barry Mussenden, project worker with Sia, the national development agency for the black voluntary sector. Sia organises conferences, training courses, seminars, consultation meetings and launches (amongst other events).

You might find it helpful to divide your target audience into your primary and secondary audience. The primary audience is the crucial group. It contains those people you want to attend as delegates, customers, etc. The secondary audience is also important. It contains those people who should know about the event but who might not necessarily attend (journalists, key opinion formers, supporters, sponsors, etc). Those people who make up the secondary audience for one event could well be the primary audience for another and vice versa. So it's important to be clear exactly who you're targeting for each individual event.

In defining your target audience these are the characteristics you might consider:

- their geographical location: are you targeting nationally, regionally or locally?
- their organisation: are you aiming for specific individuals, or for people as representatives of particular organisations?
- the communities they are part of or represent: in order to reach black and ethnic communities effectively you should, according to Sia's Barry Mussenden: *"look at translation and interpretation if you want community members and management committee members there rather than just workers and professionals"*
- their status within an organisation: are you going for senior managers, chief executives, etc for operational staff, or for a representative deemed appropriate by the organisation?
- numbers and potential numbers: how many people do you want to attract to your event? Does your defined target audience give you a large enough potential number to draw on?
- availability and timetabling: will your target audience be able to spend the time required to attend your event? Have you allowed sufficient time for them to book it into their diaries?

It's all very well defining your target audience — the people you ideally want to attend your event. Do they want to come along? What evidence do you have that the target audience either wants or needs an event of the kind you're proposing? If they don't have anything to gain or any desire to attend then you won't get anyone attending!

EVENT FORMAT DESIGN

Your event plan will need to include details of the format and timetable you intend to use. This will enable you to find appropriate venues, speakers, etc and budget accordingly.

The factors that will influence your event format cover:

- the purpose of the event (aims and objectives, etc)
- the size and nature of the target audience
- likely available budget.

The main types of event are covered later in the book and these include:

- auctions
- balls, dinners and themed evenings
- conferences
- exhibitions and displays
- fairs and fêtes
- festivals
- fundraising special events
- open days
- openings/launches
- press conferences/photo opportunities
  protests, demonstrations and vigils
- seminars, workshops and training days.

THE DATE

When are you going to hold your event? For some people the answer is easy — it's an annual event and it's always on the Saturday closest to 2 June, for example. Others have to select a date and this can be slightly more scientific than sticking a pin in the calendar.

"The day and date of the event is important," says Artswork's Ruth Jones. *"Your target group may not turn up to a weekend event, for instance. Young*

Organising Effective Events

people cannot attend a week day event unless they are in the holidays. Then they have Saturday jobs, sports and other commitments. Sundays are difficult because of transport. And people won't turn up for an early start."

Ruth adds: *"People who are expected to turn up because it's their duty due to work, etc would prefer office hours. Volunteers have other day jobs and cannot get time off, so may prefer evenings or weekends. You can't please all the people all the time, but you can certainly do a bit of research and find the best option."*

If you want to ensure you reach black and minority communities effectively then Sia's Barry Mussenden recommends: *"Avoid long events during the 40 days of Ramadan, when people will be fasting (particularly avoid all day events where lunch is to be served. If an all day event is to be held on a Friday, provision should be made for Muslim prayer (whether through an extended lunchbreak to allow time to visit a Mosque or through a private room that can be used for prayer. And be mindful of religious festivals such as Diwali (in October) for both Hindus and Sikhs."*

Some further questions you might ask when deciding on a date are listed below.

Which year? Believe it or not you might ask this question. Perhaps you want to hold an anniversary event. Then you need to be clear which anniversary you are celebrating and triple check that you are going for the correct year.

Which season? You might want to avoid the summer because people will be away on holiday. Alternatively summer might be just the right time because of the weather conditions. You might want to avoid winter because of the disruption around Christmas and the unpredictable weather. Then again, winter might be precisely the right time for a "Holly and Ivy Ball".

Which month? Now you are focusing on the appropriate month you will need to consider other activities that your organisation is involved in, the amount of time you need to attract people to the event and similar issues.

General Principles and Issues

Which week? You will probably want to avoid half term holidays and religious festivals, unless your event is specifically connected to these. At this stage you might need to do a bit of research to see if there are any exhibitions, conferences and other events that your target audience could already be committed to — and avoid these dates.

Which day? There are arguments for and against picking almost any day or days in the week. Fridays, for instance, can be good for training days because people can plan for a four-day week in the office and prepare for a final relaxing and stimulating day at your event. A Friday event gives people the chance to get away early for the weekend. Then again, the problems of the week mount up and need to be sorted out before the weekend — causing cancellations. Travelling on a Friday isn't particularly pleasant either.

A mid-week event means people can sort out problems at the beginning of the week and know they still have a couple of days in the office after your event too. On the other hand, once you get into the flow of work for the week it can be hard to schedule the time to take a day out in the middle.

Weekends can be good because you aren't competing with other work demands. But people value their leisure time!

What time of day? If you are going for an all-day event then you need to think about appropriate start and finish times. You need to allow people time to arrive, depending on the location and where they are travelling from. And you need to allow them to get away in reasonable time to avoid the rush hour. But you also want to give them value for money by packing in as much as possible in the time available.

If you are running an evening event, then you need to consider whether people are going to come straight from work or whether to allow them time to go home and eat first, etc.

Whatever you decide on will be right for some delegates and problematic for others. So you need to be clear about why you have decided on the particular time and date and be able to explain this to them should they ask.

BRANDING AND THEMES

Having decided on the format and date for your event, you now need to come up with an event "identity". The following are some of the things you should consider.

An event name/title
The title should be fairly short and snappy and should convey what the event is all about. You might like to incorporate the name of your charity into the event title to remind people that you are behind the activity.

A house-style for printed materials
It might be appropriate to simply use your own letterhead and organisation's logo on printed materials. However, many event organisers find it helpful to develop specific event-related letterheads, brochures and logos to create an event brand. For some this helps to build up audience loyalty, if they are running a series of related events. Others want to create a particular image for a one-off event.

The theme of the event
Your theme might already be decided. If you are running a conference, exhibition or training day, for example, you will already know what the focus of the event is. It's very unlikely that you'll simply say: "Let's organise a conference next year. Right, now, what shall we have a conference about?"

It's much more likely that you will say, for example: "Our research shows that there are a number of organisations providing exemplary childcare packages for their employees. But there are still huge gaps, particularly when you look at small businesses. How can we encourage

General Principles and Issues

employers to share best practice and explore the options open to them. Ah, yes, let's consider a conference..." There you have your theme.

Equally with training events, protests, press conferences and exhibitions, you are probably setting up the event in response to a perceived need. That identified need will form the theme for the event.

If, though, you decide to run a fundraising dinner, for example, you might need to come up with a theme. This could be anything from a Wild West evening through to an Ugly Bugs ball. The main purpose of this sort of theme is to be fun and to get people along. It's an area that needs brainstorming and you need to be sure that everyone is comfortable with the theme you decide on.

Annual events — AGMs, festivals, fairs, etc — can also benefit from being given a theme. Your AGM, for instance, might be focused around a particular campaign theme from the past year. Or it might have a broad theme (like political party conferences) such as "working together". This gives you a particular perspective that will help to link a variety of presentations together. For instance, your fundraiser could talk about "working together with companies and local government". Your volunteer co-ordinator could talk about "working together with the local community". Your campaigns manager could talk about "working together with the media", etc.

An annual festival will probably have a similar theme each year, but it's refreshing to give it a new twist. Changing the emphasis slightly helps to keep participants interested and audiences attending. An annual young poets festival, for example, already has a broad theme — young people's poetry. But you might want to give the whole event another theme such as "The Family" or "My Community".

Fairs, fêtes and jumble sales, etc might have no theme whatsover, other than a fair for your charity. Again, though, adding a theme such as a "St Trinians Fair" can make the event much more fun for those taking part as stallholders and more attractive to people who might attend.

Budget and pricing

As with all projects, your event needs to be thoroughly budgeted and

Organising Effective Events

should include a cost for your time. You might come up with draft costings under the following headings.

People/time
- organisation and administration
- speechwriting/copywriting
- speakers/VIPs
- travel and expenses.

Venue
- room hire/delegate fee
- refreshments
- audio visual, sets, staging.

Printed material
- design
- printing
- photocopying.

Access
- translation and interpretation
- induction loops, sign language interpreters
- personal assistance
- crêche
- travel/transport assistance.

Materials
- badges
- signage.

Marketing and promotions
- postage
- telemarketing
- advertising
- media liaison
- photography.

General
- overheads
- insurance
- management fee (possibly).

Other possible expenditure
- celebrity
- entertainment.

As Charlotte Macpherson of the NCVO says: *"Allow in the budget for extra hidden costs that invariably occur."*

Once you have worked out the draft costs (with or without VAT as appropriate) you can start to think about pricing. If you are fortunate and have a sponsor to support the event then this is less of an issue, although many sponsors part-fund and part-underwrite events (guaranteeing to meet any shortfall in income).

The price per delegate or attendee will depend mainly on:

- the perceived value of the event
- what the delegate can and is prepared to afford
- the total costs of the event
- the number of anticipated delegates.

It is worth doing some research into pricing. Take a look at what people are being charged to attend similar events — are these events attracting the sort of people you want? Talk to some of your contacts about what they would be prepared to pay. And find out from your sponsor if they are happy with the proposed price — because they are going to be closely associated with the event and some delegates might say they should provide a larger delegate subsidy.

RESPONSIBILITIES/LINES OF COMMAND

Your event plan should outline who is responsible for different elements of the event, and who is ultimately "in charge".

General Principles and Issues

might also want to make a note of enquiries so that you can evaluate your promotional material and include additional details in future marketing.

If your event requires advance booking then you will need to set up a delegate database and protocols to handle their reservations. Your database will probably include the following fields:

- delegate name and salutation
- job title
- organisation
- address
- phone and fax numbers (and e-mail address)
- date of booking
- payment received/invoiced
- dates of further correspondence
- any dietary requirements
- any communications requirements
- any access requirements
- any other comments.

You will need to decide how you want to acknowledge a booking and you might want to set yourself a target of replying within three working days.

Delegates could be sent a postcard or a standard letter with a map of how to get to the event. They could be sent a questionnaire relating to any dietary, access or communications requirements at this stage. You might want to send further event details or information about specific activities workshops. Or there might be an event brochure that you issue once people have registered.

Some event organisers prefer to send an initial acknowledgement and then more details nearer to the date of the event itself. This is because the final mailing acts as a reminder and prompts people who are going to cancel to get in touch.

MARKETING AND PROMOTION

"Nothing beats word of mouth guerilla tactics," says Artswork's Ruth Jones. *"I know my target audiences and I call them up, write by hand, talk to them in the street and generally never miss an opportunity to plug at other events — through posters and flyers, for example."*

All of the planning activities described so far are part of the marketing mix. It's also important to consider some additional ways of attracting people to your event, ie a clown on stilts with a promotional sandwich board or a personal invitation delivered by a town crier or the more traditional and straightforward approaches.

This book, though, is not the place to give a detailed guide to marketing techniques. Instead it gives pointers and prompts to some of the more obvious considerations for event organisers.

Mailings

Targeted mailings can be a great way of reaching potential participants. Such mailings are only as good, though, as the database they are based on. The database, usually compiled for another purpose, will normally more or less accurately target those people you want to invite to your event.

For your AGM, for instance, you will have a thorough knowledge of your members and you'll be able to work from your own records to invite precisely the right people. The only wasted invites will be those sent to people who've moved address without telling you. Similarly if you are running a follow up to a previous event you can mail all of those who attended your earlier one. Both of these examples are within your control and of guaranteed relevance.

However, if you are trying to reach other people through a mailing then you might need to do a bit of research to find appropriate databases. If you are targeting other charities, for instance, you might buy labels from relevant councils or voluntary services. If you are inviting people from local businesses the relevant local authority may have mailing labels or databases on disk. Yellow Pages also produce labels and databases according to different business categories and geographical locations. These are just some examples of sources, but you will need to assess how relevant such databases are and whether your budget can afford them.

Another issue to consider is whether your mailings should be available in other languages. *"But,"* says Sia's Barry Mussenden, *"even more important than translation is dissemination — there is no use in producing glossy translated leaflets if the target audience never gets to see them. As well as targeting black voluntary organisations, you should target community groups, including places of worship such as Mosques, Gudwaras, Temples, Black Churches, etc. And if you are using translated publicity material do so in all the main local community languages not just one."*

Posters

If you are running an event targeting a broad cross-section of the local community then posters can be a useful promotional tool. Posters are also a good way of highlighting your event within your organisation. They can be used effectively if your target audience regularly meets in, or visits, a limited number of buildings (such as youth centres, doctors' surgeries, etc).

You can't simply go round flyposting though. Remember to ask for permission to put up posters. And ensure that the posters give as much information as is necessary without being too cluttered and busy. The essentials are obviously the name of the event, venue and time, contact for further information and booking details (if necessary). Then you need to make the poster eyecatching without misleading. The poster needs to "sell" your event at a glance.

Editorial

Many local newspapers and radio stations have slots where you can promote community events. There's no guarantee that your event will get a mention because you will be competing with lots of other organisations for coverage. These sorts of slots simply give a one-sentence description of the event and contact details.

To find out what opportunities are available locally you will need to look through your local newspapers and listen to both BBC and independent radio. You might be able to make your event slightly more newsworthy so that you get more prominent coverage. Again, there are no guarantees, so treat editorial as a welcome extra rather than your only means of promotion.

You will need to send out a news release that is punchy and interesting. You're unlikely to get any decent coverage if you simply say: "The Little Tots Playgroup is holding a workshop for other playgroup leaders on 16 June." You might get a line in one of the community slots, but little more.

However, if you start your release: "Local playgroup leaders will be dressing up and digging in the sandpit at a workshop on 'Learning through Play' on 16 June..." What you have done with this opening is to make the event more interesting to the general reader, not just the people who might want to attend the event. An editor is going to be more inclined to run the story. They might not, though, include contact details for people who want to attend or say that there are still places available at the workshop. You might get some good awareness raising coverage but at the same time no additional delegates.

Advertising

If you pay to advertise your event then you know exactly who you are targeting, when the advert will appear, what size it will be, etc. Below are some of the issues you'll need to consider if you are thinking of advertising:

- how appropriate is the medium you are proposing to use?
- how accurately does it target your potential audience? How much "wasteage" will there be (for example, readers that aren't potential delegates)?
- how much does it cost and can your budget stand this?
- is it value for money (numbers reached per money spent)?

If you are targeting a specific group of professionals, then a trade press advert might be appropriate. Talk to a few potential delegates to find out what they and most of their colleagues read.

If you are going for the local community you might want to advertise in parish magazines — but you'll need to ensure you fit in with their deadlines (particularly if their magazines are bi-monthly).

Telephone marketing

If you are looking for a small number of people to attend your event (if it's a consultative meeting with a group of key opinion formers, for instance, or if you are running a high cost and high value training event) then you might find it worthwhile to "sell" the event over the phone. There are specialist telemarketing firms which can work to a supplied script and can sell your event for you. But, if you have staff or volunteers who are willing and available, this is often preferable. They will know all about the event, be committed to it and their enthusiasm will sing through over the phone.

Most people won't simply decide to attend on the basis of your phone call, though. They will ask for more information in writing. You might view the phone call as a way of alerting people to your event so that when they receive a written invitation they make the connection — and spend a little longer looking at it than if it were received "cold".

Word of mouth

The final way of reaching your target audience is through "word of mouth". It could be your own mouth! You might tell people about the event at official and informal meetings. But you can only reach a limited number of people.

You can ask staff and volunteers to spread the word. Ultimately, word of mouth is a good way of stimulating interest that needs to be followed up with further written information. You need to prompt people to act (book a place, for example) or possibly give them a written reminder for their desk or mantlepiece.

TIMETABLES

Your event plan needs a detailed timetable. You might include ideal and absolute deadlines for every action, or you might prefer an approach that says what outcomes are to be achieved on a weekly basis. However you draw up your timetable it's important to continually refer to it and, if necessary, revise it. You might set your timetable out on a spreadsheet so that it's easy to adapt. Or you might put it up on a wallchart so that you can see it each day.

If you circulate a timetable to colleagues, then it's useful to highlight those actions or outcomes that are their responsibility. Ask them to let you know if these timings are realistic, and make sure they tell you if there is likely to be any slippage.

ON-THE-DAY-STAFFING

The final ingredient in the event plan is an outline of your staffing plans for the day/s. Obviously the scale of your event will dictate the numbers of helpers/organisers that are needed, but some of the areas to consider are:

- setting up, signage
- venue liaison, room layouts
- audio visual equipment
- access and communictions requirements
- car parking
- registration
- refreshments and dietary requirements
- VIPs, workshop leaders and speakers
- media liaison
- keeping the event to time
- troubleshooting and delegate assistance
- health and safety.

SUMMARY

An event plan is a "living document'. Don't just file it away (though even thinking things through is useful). Involve others in compiling the event plan, circulate the working version, and send round updates as things change.

LEARNING FROM OTHERS

Once you've organised a couple of exhibitions or conferences you begin to know what to look out for — the potential problems and the extra ingredients that really lift the event. But if it's your first such event the whole thing can seem quite overwhelming. That's why it's important to talk to other event organisers.

You might be an experienced workshop co-ordinator, but how would you feel about running a festival? You might have put on lots of fundraising spectaculars, but would you know how to set up a good

AGM? Research and networking are essential. You might be able to talk to someone within your own company who has organised particular events in the past. They can help by providing lots of background written information as well as running through what works and what doesn't.

You might need to liaise with other organisations too. You might know about a different aspect of event organisation that would be useful to them. If this is the case, an informal chat might suffice. Or you might want to set up something more formal like a training session or mentoring arrangement. The most important thing, though, is not to struggle to re-invent the whole process on your own. It's just too time-consuming and risky.

VENUE HIRE AND LIAISON

Most events involve hiring a venue — unless you are lucky enough to have purpose-built meeting rooms of your own. In this section it's assumed that you have to hire the facilities to put on your event. (It is important that event venues are accessible for disabled people and this is covered in depth in the next section.)

What issues do you need to consider when looking for a venue?

THE TYPE OF VENUE

When you start to look for a suitable venue for your event you will already have a clear idea of the event format and the numbers of people you are hoping for. It's worth developing a quick checklist based on this information. Then you can send this through to potential venues or venue finding organisations. Some of the things that you might include in such a checklist are:

General Principles and Issues

- location (this might be more or less tightly defined)
- transport links (proximity to public transport, motorways, etc)
- car parking facilities (either on-site or nearby. If nearby, the price might be important and might need to be stated in delegate information)
- venue type (this will depend on your type of event and delegate expectations — it could be anything from a four star hotel, purpose-built conferencing facilities or a university to a community centre, field and marquee or aircraft hangar)
- number and size of rooms (in addition you will need to ensure that rooms can be set out in the configuration you are looking for — for instance a room that can sit 10 people theatre style might not be appropriate if you are running a workshop and need a room for 10 people sitting in a friendly U-shape)
- internal layout of the venue (if you want to hire a main conference room and four breakout rooms you probably want them to be in the same area within the venue rather than spread out over a campus)
- registration area (you need a large enough area near to the venue entrance so that delegates aren't squashed in a queue or in danger of getting lost before they have arrived)
- refreshment area and arrangements (you should be clear about whether delegates all need to be seated for lunch, for instance. You also should find out what sort of menus are available. Sadly, it is often the refreshments that make a venue either unaffordable or disappointing
- audio visual equipment (if the venue does not have what you need you should be able to hire this from a local firm — check to see if the venue has regular suppliers)
- adequate toilet facilities near to your hired rooms (otherwise some delegates miss out on networking opportunities in refreshment breaks and only have the opportunity to talk to the next person in the queue for the loo!)
- price/delegate fee (in some cases it is cheaper to pay for room hire

and then refreshments on top, in other instances an all-in delegate fee is more economical. Most venues will negotiate)
- availability on dates required.

In addition, you need to assess whether or not the staff are friendly, helpful and supportive enough. You will need to be in regular contact in the run up to the event and it's essential that they are responsive and easy to deal with. When it comes to the event itself you will want them to be on-hand and involved, so their manner is very important.

HOW DO YOU FIND A VENUE?

There are a number of organisations that help to find venues. You simply give them your criteria and they come up with a selection of more or less appropriate venues. They make their money through a commission from the venue you select. There are also CD-ROMS and directories produced by organisations such as the British Association of Conference Towns (BACT). There are also tourist information officers who can send you local conference packs and who can fax around venues in their area to see if any meet your criteria.

This all helps with your initial research. Personal recommendations are another useful source of information. Even when you've come up with a list of, say, three potential venues you shouldn't make a decision until you've been to see them for yourself.

Venues are keen for business. Their conference co-ordinators can sometimes work too hard to make the venue fit your criteria. They might not point out that to provide four conference break-out areas means dividing up one large room which isn't soundproofed. They are unlikely to tell you that the rooms are tatty and the staff unhelpful! There really is no substitute for assessing the venue yourself.

General Principles and Issues

UNUSUAL VENUES

Listed below are just some of the more unusual types of venues that are becoming available for event hire. Because many of them have other purposes they will need to be checked even more thoroughly to ensure they are suitable for your event:

- beaches and piers
- boats/ferries
- castles and country houses
- museums and galleries
- racetracks and railways
- theme parks
- wildlife parks
- working venues (vineyards, mills, sweet-makers, etc).

Local tourist information offices will be able to provide you with details of what is available in your area.

VENUE LIAISON

Once you have decided on your perfect venue, you need to confirm everything in writing. If possible your letter of confirmation should cover:

- date/s hired and any cancellation charges/scale
- car parking facilities, particularly if any areas are to be reserved
- all rooms and areas booked, internal signage arrangements, and the position with any shared public areas you are using
- access, communications and special dietary requirements (more details are given below)
- audio visual arrangements (either equipment hired from the venue or hired from an external supplier)
- setting up and departure times

Organising Effective Events

- help provided by venue staff
- registration and cloakroom arrangements
- refreshments (numbers may still need to be confirmed)
- full details of the costs and any additional items that may need to be booked (eg flipcharts, OHPs, etc)
- overnight accommodation arrangements
- room layouts
- any additional changes or arrangements the venue has promised to make before your event.

Take this letter along to the event with you and then if any problems arise you can refer to your agreement. Venue management is a high turnover industry and conference co-ordinators frequently change jobs. You will often find yourself dealing with a number of different people at the venue. Furthermore, when you are setting up for your event you will usually be liaising with the duty manager rather than the conference co-ordinator so it helps to have everything agreed in writing.

As the event gets closer you will need to liaise with the venue to remind them of what has been agreed, to advise them of any changes, to give them a detailed event timetable, and to let them know delegate numbers.

Good venues pride themselves on meeting your every need and ensuring your event runs smoothly. But it is safer to assume that at least one or two things won't be as you anticipated. Allow yourself plenty of setting up time, establish who is in charge and have some contingency plans ready. This isn't to say that you should be really negative about your event. However, if you expect everything to be as promised then when things aren't quite right you can feel incredibly stressed. If you anticipate the need for a couple of tweaks then you should be able to deal with them energetically and efficiently. The secret is to leave yourself plenty of time to sort things out, and to have helpers on hand so that you can devote yourself to one thing at a time.

General Principles and Issues

EQUALITY OF ACCESS

"Disabled people are after the same access to events as others. They don't want to be treated as special cases that have to be cared for. They simply want to fully participate as delegates or speakers," says Brian Hicks of the BCODP (British Council of Organisations of Disabled People). *"Unfortunately, people are disabled by the barriers that exist in our society,"* he adds. *"By physical barriers and the attitudes of other people."*

This section looks at some of the ways in which event organisers can try to tackle these barriers. First, a general warning from Brian Hicks: *"Event organisers shouldn't just accept it when a venue says they're accessible. Very often a venue says it's accessible because it has a lift or one accessible toilet. But there can be hidden problems like a lift that's too small for electronic wheelchairs or one that doesn't have room for someone's personal assistant."*

Every event organiser needs, then, to visit their venue and consider a whole range of issues (see below). It's really hard for a non-disabled person to spot all of the potential problems and to ensure that appropriate facilities are in place. If you are worried then it's worth consulting a local organisation of disabled people for further advice.

Before considering the issues involved, if disabled people are invited to attend your event as *delegates*, what do you need to address if you are inviting a disabled person to *speak* at an event? All of the issues relating to accessibility that are important for delegates are applicable if one of your speakers is a disabled person. However, you also need to think about some of the following.

PERSONAL ASSISTANCE

If you are paying a fee to a disabled person, then you might also need to offer a fee so that they can be supported by a personal assistant. The PA will need accommodation and refreshments, etc too.

STAGING

What sort of staging is there if any? If there is a raised platform, is there an appropriate ramp up to it for wheelchair users? Is there someone to guide a visually impaired speaker? But most importantly ask your speaker where they would prefer to be. Would they rather speak from the floor? Give them options.

Also consider how your speakers will arrive on stage and their exit. Either all speakers should be on the set awaiting the delegates' entrance or none should be. You shouldn't have one wheelchair user on stage with three empty chairs for other speakers!

MICROPHONES

If your speaker is going to address the audience from the floor, or if they are going to be speaking on stage from a wheelchair, then consider the height of the microphones. It's embarrassing and very unprofessional to fiddle about with microphones in the middle of proceedings. You might need to book additional microphones so that they can be set up ready.

SENSORY CONSIDERATIONS

If your speaker has a *hearing* impairment, then remember:

- an induction loop will need to encircle your speaker too, if it is appropriate and they are to benefit from it
- you might need to book an additional sign language interpreter to sign for your speaker/s if they are sitting on the stage during other speeches
- you might need to book an interpreter to provide "voice over" for your speaker.

General Principles and Issues

If your speaker has a *visual* impairment, then the following points should be borne in mind:

- if other speakers are using visual aids you will need to convey these to your speaker (through large print handouts, Braille, description, etc)
- you should ask your speaker how much preparation time they would like in getting accustomed to the layout of the room and the stage set-up.

Many issues are applicable to both speakers and delegates.

PHYSICAL ACCESSIBILITY

One of the first questions to ask is: "How accessible is the venue?" This means more than erecting a ramp.

CAR PARKING

Think about how good the parking facilities are. Are they near to the venue? Are there any appropriate spaces reserved for orange badge holders? If not can you reserve an area yourself? Once you have answered these questions then it's important to communicate the details to any relevant delegates so they know what to expect and can arrive in good time for the event.

Clear and honest communication is vital at all times. If a situation is less than perfect don't claim "all facilities are fully accessible". You might need to say "there are three car parking spaces reserved for orange badge holders, other parking is available in the adjacent car park". That way people's expectations aren't disappointed.

ENTRANCE AND REGISTRATION AREA

The next thing to look at is the venue entrance and registration area. Many venues have a small step up to the doorway, although more modern buildings are either at the same level or have an appropriate ramp. Although this is the first thing to look out for, it's not the only thing to consider.

Also take a look at the doorway itself and then assess the area you are going to use for registration. Is it large enough for people to move around comfortably? Is there enough seating? Are there places to put cups of coffee down? Will the registration desk be at an appropriate height?

MOVING ROUND THE VENUE

Often within a venue there are split levels, with short flights of steps. Sometimes there are a couple of steps into syndicate rooms. You need to look around all rooms you are going to use — including the restaurant and other breakout areas. Another issue to consider is the carpeting. A thick pile means it's harder for wheelchair users to maneouvre.

It's also good to have an overview to the whole venue and how delegates move around. Are conference, breakout areas, syndicate rooms, toilets, etc close together?

LIFTS

If people are moving between levels in a venue then a lift is vital, but even lifts need to be checked out. If the only available lift is a goods lift then you need to think carefully about whether this is an appropriate venue. Sadly, sometimes local facilities are thin on the ground and you have to compromise. But if you do need to use a venue with a goods

General Principles and Issues

lift then the following are essential: you need to have staff on hand at all times to open and close doors and operate the lift; the lift needs to be near to all the appropriate rooms (not on the other side of the venue); access to the lift needs to be clear (not through a storeroom, for instance); and delegates need to be told about the situation in advance.

Some lifts are very small. If they are too small then the larger electronic wheelchairs may not fit. If this is a concern you may need to ask a disabled person to check this out for you. Also consider whether the lift can accommodate another person at the same time as the wheelchair user — so that a personal assistant, for instance can help to operate the lift.

ACCESSIBLE TOILETS

If a number of disabled people are attending your event then you need to consider whether there are enough accessible toilets. If your event is in an hotel where there is just one toilet for disabled people you might ask the venue to open up a couple of its bedrooms for disabled people. Again you need to consider where these toilet facilities are in relation to the rest of your event.

EVENT ROOMS

Accessibility inside rooms is just as important as outside. If you are holding an exhibition then you need to ensure that there is sufficient aisle space for wheelchair users to move around freely. Exhibitions shouldn't be on raised platforms. It should go without saying, there mustn't be any trailing wires. Carpeting again is an important consideration.

If you are organising a presentation to delegates in a theatre style arrangement then don't force wheelchair users into one area. Give them the freedom to choose whether or not they want to be at the front, the back or anywhere else in the room by providing enough space throughout. If you are dealing with a room with fixed seating (in a university, for instance) this won't be possible. Let delegates know if this is the case.

If delegates are going into workshop/syndicate groups, then ensure there is enough room for wheelchair users. Often venues try to squeeze large numbers into small rooms (often converted bedrooms). Make sure people can fit in comfortably and that there's room to move around for pair work, for example.

REFRESHMENTS

Refreshments and special diets are examined in more detail below, but it's worth noting that *"buffets can be one of the most horrific times for disabled people,"* according to Brian Hicks of the BCODP. *"When you've got to hold a plate and a cup it can be inhibiting beyond belief."* Buffet organisers should always ensure there are at least some seats and tables available.

Another thing to consider about buffets is how they are served. Some disabled people might not be able to get as near to the food as other delegates and so you should have additional serving staff on hand to assist. The serving staff should be briefed to be available to help with a positive attitude. They shouldn't thrust food at disabled delegates, but be ready to assist.

To avoid embarrassment for everyone concerned, it's worth finding out if any help is required with cutting up food, etc in advance.

OVERNIGHT

If you are organising a residential event then there are a number of further considerations.

Many hotels now have one or more accessible rooms with large bedrooms and bathrooms, and they include a range of adaptations. However, if — like the BCODP's annual conference — you are looking for a hotel with anything up to 50 rooms that are appropriate for wheelchair users then it can be hard to find a suitable venue. The BCODP uses the Stakis Hotel at Northampton for its annual conference.

Event organiser, Brian Hicks, explains: *"Whilst only three of the rooms are specially adapted, most of the bedrooms are accessible. The problem with many hotels is the bathroom. But at the Stakis there is plenty of room to move a wheelchair around in the bathroom and to position it next to the toilet so that you can transfer out of the chair onto the loo. The staff at the hotel are great, they have a 'no problem' attitude and there are plenty on hand ready to help when asked.*

The most important thing, though, is to explain clearly to delegates what is and isn't available. If you're up-front about the facilities then people have the appropriate expectations."

Listed below are some of the things to look out for if you are organising an overnight residential event.

1. All the access issues that you'd look out for in organising a day event (level entry into the hotel, door and corridor width, carpet pile, internal steps/ramps, size of lift and positioning of lift controls, sufficient numbers of helpful and aware staff, space in refreshment areas, etc).
2. Large bedrooms with sufficient room to manoeuvre (even the largest modern electronic wheelchair), and wide enough doorways into the room and internally.
3. Large bathrooms with sufficient room to manoeuvre and space beside the toilet for a wheelchair to be positioned (ie no bidet adjacent to the toilet).
4. Either baths with pulleys or bars, or appropriate washing facilities (and if a bath isn't available make sure you brief delegates about the washing facilities before their arrival).

Some further issues to consider when you are making sure that your events are accessible to all delegates are as follows.

Organising Effective Events

SENSORY IMPAIRMENTS

Delegates who have hearing or visual impairments might have some specific requirements (see below). First, though, a general point about health and safety — check with the venue about their health and safety arrangements, particularly the issue of fire alarms and emergency procedures. Make sure you give this information to delegates at the beginning of the event.

Deaf people use a variety of means of communication, and individuals may choose one or more methods that they feel happy and comfortable with. The Deaf Community, for instance, has its own language — British Sign Language (BSL). Deaf people and deafened people might use hearing aids and lipreading, etc. You shouldn't make assumptions about how to make your event accessible. You need to ask the individual concerned. Some of the things that might make your event accessible include:

- sign language interpreters
- an induction loop
- notetaker/s
- hearing dogs.

Sign language interpreters

One sign language interpreter is rarely enough, unless your event is very brief. Interpreting is a complex and tiring process. The interpreter needs to listen very carefully to what is said, get the meaning, translate it into BSL in their heads, and then sign the meaning.

Even if your event only involves a 30 minute presentation there are other issues to consider such as the networking and refreshment times. It is likely that you will need two or more interpreters. When you book the interpreter and explain the nature of your event they can give you further advice. The Council for the Advancement of Communication with Deaf People (CACDP) produces a directory listing qualified sign language interpreters. The RNID, RAD and various other local organisations for deaf people provide sign language interpreter booking services. Most of these agencies will also provide you with notes on how to use sign language interpreters effectively. It helps if you can provide plenty of background briefing information about the event and the topics for discussion. Speakers' notes and delegate packs are also useful so that the interpreter can familiarise themselves with the issues.

It's also useful to put the interpreters and delegates in touch in advance. They can liaise about things like where to meet and when, and any particular requirements. Speakers and workshop leaders should be briefed in advance on how to use sign language interpreters. Speakers will need to consider the speed of their delivery. Workshop leaders will need to ensure people don't all speak at once.

Lighting is another important issue to consider. Interpreters need to be able to stand in front of a plain background (without sunlight blazing in through the curtains and without busy distracting backdrops, for example). The lighting should be crisp enough for delegates to focus on the interpreter easily.

Induction loops are helpful if people use hearing aids. The induction loop, in combination with a hearing aid, cuts down on background noise and amplifies the speaker's voice. Many venues — such as theatres and hotels — are installing induction loops into their main rooms. You can also buy or hire portable loop systems to lay out yourself (if you do this then you will probably need to tape down the wiring or use some other way of ensuring delegates aren't in danger of tripping up). If you are using induction loops:

- ensure that all those who want to use the loop are encircled by it (ie don't exclude speakers at a top table)
- inform delegates in advance if the loop system will be available and ensure they know it is there on the day so that they can switch their hearing aids to the appropriate "T" position

- get someone with a hearing aid to test the loop out to ensure that it is working, and be ready to sort the loop out if it is not working
- if you are hiring or using a portable loop, be sure that you know how to set it up
- make sure all speakers are aware that there is a loop system and use appropriate microphones

Notetakers are used by some people so that they can concentrate on either lipreading or the sign language interpreter. You should find out from delegates in advance if they intend to bring a notetaker — because you will need to know of the additional names and numbers for seating and refreshments. As with signers, try to supply them with as much advance briefing material as possible.

Hearing dogs are used by some deaf people for support. Check that the venue is able to accommodate dogs and that arrangements are made for the dogs' refreshments.

Some of your delegates may have visual impairments. Again their requirements will be personal to them, and you should avoid assumptions about what support to provide. To avoid embarrassment on both sides, speak with them in advance to discover what is appropriate. Some of the areas to consider are:

- personal assistants — will they be accompanied at the event by a personal assistant?
- taking notes — will they have a notetaker or will they want tapes of the speakers/workshops?
- travel — do any special arrangements need to be made for travel or arrival and departure?
- venue layout — are there any hazards in the layout of the venue to sort out? Does the delegate want a member of staff to accompany them as they move round the venue? Do they want to arrive early to familiarise themselves with the venue? Would they like to be sent a large print plan of the venue in advance?
- guide dogs — as with hearing dogs, check with the venue to ensure that it can accommodate dogs. Also check with the delegate about

whether the dog needs a rest area or any refreshments, etc. Don't assume, though, that because someone is blind that they automatically have a guide dog
- delegate materials — in what format would the delegate like their materials? On audio cassette? In large print? In Braille? Discuss with them the best way of providing materials in this way.

When it comes to making events accessible organisers often consider wheelchair users and people with sensory impairments. They less often think of people with learning difficulties or survivors of mental health problems.

LEARNING DIFFICULTIES

The BCODP is currently looking into making delegate materials accessible to people with learning difficulties by using pictures. It's a difficult area and organisations such as People First (tel: 0171-713 6400) can give more advice. Some delegates might bring along an advocate or support worker. If so, consult with them in advance about how to provide appropriate materials and how to deliver speeches/ workshops in an effective way. Find out what they want to get from the event and then work with them to ensure that you can provide this.

SURVIVORS OF MENTAL HEALTH PROBLEMS

Delegates who have had mental health problems ("survivors") may find particular workshop leaders intimidating, or they might be overwhelmed by the pace of an event. Once again, it's important to stress that every single delegate has their own individual needs and one shouldn't make assumptions. Present delegates with clear information about the nature of the event in advance. Find out as much as you can

Organising Effective Events

in advance about how you can make the event as accessible and enjoyable as possible for them.

INFORMATION AND CHOICE ARE VITAL

There are many issues, then, to consider in making an event accessible to disabled people. Some of the factors need to be considered in selecting suitable venues (even before you know who is going to be attending). Other issues will arise as people book themselves into your event and you need to be ready to ask the right questions and to provide appropriate facilities and support.

As the BCODP's Brian Hicks summarises: *"If you have any worries or doubts about accessibility talk to organisations of disabled people and to delegates themselves. And try to sort things out in advance. It's better to be prepared than to be racing round on the day saying 'Can I do this? Can I do that?' Be honest about what you can and can't provide so that people have the right expectations."*

(We are grateful to the BCODP for their help and advice with this section.)

SPONSORSHIP

Sponsorship of an event can take a variety of forms and you might have one or more sponsors as appropriate.

CASH CONTRIBUTION

A sponsor might make a non-refundable contribution towards the costs. In this way delegates can either attend for free or their places are subsidised.

UNDERWRITING

Alternatively, a sponsor might underwrite the event — guaranteeing to cover any shortfall once costs have been deducted from income. If this is the case then it's important that you cost in your time to the original agreed budget.

MIXED FUNDING

Other sponsors might part fund and part underwrite an event. Some of their money subsidises the event and makes it affordable for delegates. The remainder is a safety net in case numbers aren't as high as anticipated.

As with any sponsorship arrangement it is vital that you set out the agreement in writing so that you are clear about:

- when to expect sponsorship income (so that you aren't cash flowing the event)
- whether monies are non-refundable or are to underwrite and cash flow the event
- what branding your sponsor expects on event literature and at the event itself (through exhibition boards, banners, etc)
- what level of involvement your sponsor wants in the event preparations (attending planning meetings, for instance, or approving literature)
- what level of involvement your sponsor wants at the event itself (participating in the main event or having staff and materials available)
- your sponsor's aims in supporting the event
- who has "editorial control" over literature, speeches, etc (will the sponsor want to vet everything? How much independence do you have?)

Organising Effective Events

- who has the final say within the sponsoring organisation and with whom should you liaise if this person isn't available?

You may be lucky enough to have developed the event idea in partnership with your sponsor. But you may be in a position where you have identified a clear need for your event, researched it thoroughly and come up with a detailed plan, and then be looking for a sponsor to help cover the costs.

As with the search for any funding you will need to approach potential sponsors in plenty of time — given that most organisations plan such budgets and spends annually. You will need to be armed with a strong written proposal and be able to identify specific benefits to the organisation/s you approach. Be clear about how much money you are asking for and on what terms — are you looking for a number of part-funders, for instance?

Involving a sponsor adds another dimension to your event, and it's essential that you keep them informed of progress and changes. Ensure that at least one of your staff is responsible for looking after sponsors and their VIP guests on the day, so that they are guided around the event and discover how well run it is and how much delegates have to gain.

Ensure that sponsors receive details of delegate evaluations, and ask what worked and what didn't for them as a sponsor. Don't forget to thank them — and to suggest any further event ideas you may have. Then meet with them for an event debrief.

DOCUMENTATION AND CORRESPONDENCE

It is important to get written confirmation for every aspect of the event. As with the need for venue details to be confirmed in writing, similar issues apply to suppliers of other services — from audio visual equipment, to flowers and catering. If you have got it in writing there should be no misunderstandings. If there is a problem you can use the letter to help sort things out.

Issue purchase orders when booking goods and services. This prevents the problem of someone giving you a verbal quote for one amount and then invoicing for another (citing the various "added extras" you didn't know about).

Delegates and speakers also need things in writing to avoid any confusion or embarrassment on the day. Issue any speakers with a written brief — outlining practical arrangements, details of the audience they will be addressing and any guidance on the areas they should cover in their speech. Clear "joining instructions" for delegates should include start and finish times, a map of how to get to the event, details of the day's agenda and any particular practical arrangements.

All letters and other relevant documents should be filed carefully. If you are ill and someone needs to keep things moving they should be able to pick up the file and understand where you are with the event. A good filing system will help you deal with invoices effectively after the event.

LEGAL ISSUES AND INSURANCE

We have already indicated that effective event organisation is all about being prepared for things going wrong. It sounds negative, but if you expect people to let you down, machinery to fail and unexpected incidents to affect you then you'll be a better event organiser. It should come as no surprise to hear that insurance and legal considerations are essential.

LEGAL ISSUES

It's worth checking every contract you sign to see if you are liable for cancellation charges, for instance, or to discover whether or not a caterer reserves the right to supply you with a different menu if ingredients aren't available. Ask what the terms and conditions are under which a service is supplied. If you don't like them, don't agree to them. Discuss, haggle and come to an agreed compromise. Most importantly, know what you are signing up to.

INSURANCE

Insurance is also crucial. Each event will have different ingredients and different risks. So the first thing you should do is to discuss the matter with an independent financial advisor. Describe your event to them in detail and again try to think of everything that could "go wrong" that you might want to insure against. Your advisor will outline the risks and costs and then you will need to decide exactly how much insurance of which kind to take out.

The main types of insurance to consider are:

- pluvious (against weather conditions preventing your event)
- public liability (in case people attending your event are hurt in some way, for instance. You might also want to insure against food poisoning, even though your caterers should have their own insurance)
- employers' liability (if you are taking staff on to help with the event)
- specific equipment/exhibition materials (against their being damaged or stolen)
- celebrity appearance (it might be worth taking out some insurance if you are relying on a "star" attraction)
- competition prize (you might want to insure against someone winning your star prize, if it's a top of the range car, for example).

General Principles and Issues

AUDIO VISUAL AND SET

"Where possible use professional providers who will deliver and replace faulty equipment, and recompense you for inefficiency. And don't assume you will know how the equipment works (or even where it switches on). Make sure someone shows you how, or is available to operate it," says Artswork's Ruth Jones.

This is good advice. If you want to use technical equipment, then it's often worth paying for a technician to set it up and to operate it. If you are booking equipment through a venue find out if they have their own in-house technician. Often venues hire in the equipment themselves and the supplier sets things up and departs before you arrive. Then if there are problems there is no-one on hand to sort them out.

Some of the equipment that might be useful as well as other issues to consider are outlined below.

MICROPHONES AND P/A SYSTEM

There are various different types of microphone — they vary in price and are appropriate in different circumstances. They include:

- lapel microcphones — which, as the name implies, are attached to your clothing (the lapel of your jacket, for instance). They are useful for the chairperson or for speakers who move about a lot and want to use their hands
- hand-held microphones — these are normally used by compères or speakers as they walk around the stage. They might use them to interview other people. They can also be used within an audience when you are inviting questions from the floor. If you are using them in this way you will need assistants to pass the microphone around, on and off switches on the microphone and protocols which you explain clearly to the audience (for instance, wait until you get the

Organising Effective Events

microphone before asking a question, and state your name and organisation first)
- fixed or stand microphones — these could be built into a lectern or might be attached to a stand. They are appropriate for speakers or performers who want to address the audience from just one position.

You will need to think about the loud speakers too. How many do you need? What sort of power/volume are you looking for? Where should these speakers be positioned? In addition, you will need to discuss the use of any induction loop at the same time as you are organising your p/a system.

The two remaining things to consider are whether or not you will want any music or sound effects, and also whether you want the proceedings tape-recorded.

AUDIO VISUAL AIDS

First, it's important to ask yourself if your audio visual (a/v) equipment is appropriate. As Sia's Barry Mussenden says: *"Sia never uses audio visual equipment unless we have good audio visual material to present — boring or irrelevant audio visuals do not enrich an event. Likewise, video recording of an event should be done professionally or not at all. Home made videos are of no use."*

OVERHEAD PROJECTORS

Overhead projectors (OHPs) are really only appropriate for presentations to small groups of people. If you are organising a large event, discourage speakers from using OHPs. The effect on a big screen is scrappy and often illegible.

OHPs are most appropriate for training sessions. If you need them for this sort of situation ensure the room is large enough for you to position the OHP effectively. Test it out thoroughly before delegates arrive so that you are clear about how to focus it. Check that the lenses are clean and the picture is as sharp as possible.

SLIDE PROJECTOR/COMPUTER SCREENS

If your speaker says that he or she wants to use slides or screens created in a presentation software package like Powerpoint, then it's worth finding out a bit more about the content before organising the equipment. Slides and computer screens can enhance a presentation if the speaker is referring to something visual like architects' plans or a simple pie chart.

If they are just being used for bullet points as a prompt for the speaker then they can actually detract from the presentation. They can slow the speaker down and, worse still, the audience (already bored) can see how many more points the presenter is planning to cover.

If there is a legitimate reason for the use of slides, then you will need to find out exactly what the speaker is using. The preferred format is 35mm, glass mounted slides. You will need to check whether or not the presenter is bringing along their own carousel. Here are some further questions to ask:

- does the speaker want two carousels so that they can mix from one slide to another?
- does the speaker want to operate the slide projector, or will they want assistance (if so, can they provide an annotated script)?
- when will the slides be available? Will there be an opportunity for a rehearsal?
- does the speaker need some "blanks" to cover particular sections of their talk or to be in place at the beginning and end of their talk?

If the speaker is using a computer-generated presentation then you will need to liaise with them over exactly what kind of equipment they need and what they are intending to bring. If they are going to bring along some of the equipment themselves then they will need to liaise closely with the venue and a/v company over compatibility, setting up times and rehearsal arrangements.

VIDEO EQUIPMENT

Whilst video makes for a higher quality presentation than slides or OHPs you still need to question whether or not it is appropriate. Video works well as a scene setter. It creates a lot of "heat not light". In other words, it is a great way to quickly generate an atmosphere, but it is not an appropriate way to convey much detailed information.

You might also make use of video equipment if you are recording people within a workshop. Some venues hire out packages which they call "role play equipment". These combine a TV monitor, video recorder, camcorder and tripod. Alternatively you might need to hire the equipment from an outside contractor. Either way these are the things that you might need to specify:

- the size of the TV monitor (large enough to be seen comfortably by all delegates)
- a tripod for the camcorder (otherwise you'll have to hold it steady for the entire time it's in use!)
- how you want to use the equipment (for instance, do you want to be able to both play VHS pre-recorded videos and show what you are filming on the monitor without having to fiddle about with wires, etc?)
- a technician to set the equipment up and to show you how to use it — and also to be on standby should anything go wrong.

General Principles and Issues

LIGHTING

There are two main lighting considerations. First, you need to think about the lighting that is part of the venue itself. If you are running workshops, for example, you need to look at how much natural light is available and what sort of artificial light is provided. If people are spending a long time trying to concentrate in artificial light this can be very tiring. What sort of lighting is there in the main meeting room? Will it need to be dimmed? Do you know where the switches are?

The second major area is specially hired-in lighting — spotlights, exhibition lights, stage lights, etc. Lighting of this kind can be quite expensive and will involve an outside contractor. Using a contractor is essential — he or she will know the power requirements, have specialist equipment and will operate within health and safety rules.

If you are making use of stage spotlights then you will usually need to hire someone to operate them. This is essential if you are going to have a "roving spotlight" that follows presenters around the stage. If you are switching between different types of lighting then you will need to draw up a lighting plot.

Exhibitions and sets can be dramatically improved with a handful of lights if they are carefully positioned. Even if you are only using lights on a small scale it is still worth hiring them through a professional provider.

EXHIBITION BOARDS/SET AND STAGING

There is a wide range of exhibition boards available. Some almost construct themselves — forming magnetic skeletons on which you "hang" lightweight panels. Others are the more traditional series of boards that you construct and then attach materials using velcro. A number of office suppliers and specialist exhibition companies offer such boards and panelling for purchase or hire. It's a question of finding out what's right for you at the right price.

Organising Effective Events

If you are putting on a conference you might want to use a set of exhibition panels as a backdrop for the speakers. This will mean that any photographs taken during the event, or any media coverage will feature details from these panels (your logo, visuals and message).

Finally, if you are creating a "set" for your speakers you will also need to consider staging. Many venues have their own staging — this can be fixed permanently in place or might be a set of blocks that are assembled as required. The great thing about the temporary block type of staging is that you have some choice over what's appropriate. You might decide to hire an alternative type of staging (perhaps lower level, for instance).

Some of the things to consider when arranging staging include:

- how many people will it need to accommodate at any one time (ie will there be a seated panel waiting their turn to speak)?
- do you need an additional raised area for speakers by a lectern?
- how do people get on and off the stage? Is there a ramp for wheelchair users?
- what sort of carpeting is there on the stage? Is the nature of this carpet, colour, etc appropriate?
- do you need to mark the edge of the stage to prevent people from falling off (if the lights are dimmed for instance)?

Remember, if you are hiring equipment from an external supplier, then get more than one quote (three is best) before agreeing to the prices charged. Prices can vary quite wildly, and most firms are prepared to negotiate an individual package rather than a per-item fee.

PETTY CASH

You will need to think about how much petty cash to have available at your event — how to secure it, how it can be used and how to ensure you have appropriate receipts.

General Principles and Issues

If you are going to allow delegates to pay on arrival rather than in advance, then you will need a supply of different coins and notes to use as change. Again, you will need somewhere safe to store the money and an accurate way of recording what you receive on the door.

CHILDCARE

If you are to make your event accessible to everyone you might need to consider offering childcare provision. If your event is taking place during normal working hours and your target audience includes people in full-time paid employment then they can probably make use of their existing childcare arrangements.

However, if you are targeting people who work part-time, shift-workers, volunteers and full-time parents, or if you are organising an event outside of normal working hours then childcare can become an important part of the event package.

Some venues, such as universities, have creches on-site. You might be able to negotiate a number of places to be reserved for your delegates. But you will need to check carefully the status of the facilities, the qualifications of the staff, the age of children they can care for and your own liability in booking the places. It can be easier to make a bursary available to pay for a certain number of delegates' childcare costs.

TRAVEL, TRANSPORT AND OVERNIGHT ACCOMMODATION

It is important not to forget your own travel, transport and overnight accommodation needs. You can be so focused on sorting out arrangements for speakers and delegates that your own needs are overlooked. Try to make these arrangements as early on as possible, then this will leave you free to concentrate on other things.

OVERNIGHT ACCOMMODATION

Even when the event you are organising is quite close by you might want to organise one or more overnights so that you are able to work late and start early. If your event is taking place in an hotel, then the obvious place to consider for overnight accommodation is the venue itself. However, it doesn't always work out as the cheapest option. Many hotels will negotiate rates for their facilities, but they won't always come down very far on bedroom prices. If you're on a tight budget you might need to stay elsewhere. You might even welcome the chance to escape for a while.

If you are looking for accommodation near to your venue then you can find local facilities through the nearest tourist information office or a specialist booking agency. One question you might want to ask is how early they will serve breakfast. There might be a set time at which the restaurant opens and this might be too late for your requirements. If so, find out if they serve breakfast to your room at an earlier time. Equally, how late in the evening do they serve dinner, and is there room service after this time?

TRAVEL AND TRANSPORT

Travel and transport can be two separate issues. The first relates to how you get to and from the venue. The second refers to how you move all the equipment and materials. If you use a delivery firm to transport all your gear then this leaves you free to use public transport or to drive with a safe load in your car. It will leave you feeling fresher as you set up, and make it easier for you to get away at the end of the

General Principles and Issues

event. You have to trust your delivery firm to deliver on time and without damaging any of the items they are transporting.

EVENT LITERATURE

Most event organisers have some sort of literature available for delegates. This can range from a glossy programme to a photocopied order of events. The format of your event literature will depend on your available budget, target audience and the nature of what is going on. However, some of the things to consider including in your event literature are:

- timings — is it clear when certain things are happening, including refreshment breaks?
- venue plan — do you need a schematic layout of the venue so that people can find their way around? Is it clear where different groups of people should go? Are the toilets and cloakrooms clearly marked?
- speakers/workshop leaders/performers — do you need to explain who is "appearing" and do you need to give any further details about them?
- handouts and delegate notes — do you need to produce handouts for specific activities or further notes for delegates to take away?
- prices — do you need to run through the prices of any goods on sale, meals, etc?
- evaluations — are you going to ask delegates to complete a written evaluation of the event? (See also below.)

Remember to think about access to this literature. Should it be available in other languages? Should it be available in large print, on tape and in Braille? Do you need to offer a pictorial version for people with learning difficulties?

THE WEATHER, HEATING AND AIR CONDITIONING

If your event is being held outside, then the weather and temperature are obvious worries. But, even if your event is being held indoors, you still need to consider these issues. It can be particularly difficult to anticipate some of the problems if your visit to the venue is at a completely different time of the year (for instance, if you view a hotel in the winter to assess it for a conference you are holding in the summer).

THE WEATHER

Rain

If it might rain, is there sufficient room for all of the umbrellas and for hanging up wet coats? Will delegates and speakers be able to find their belongings quickly at the end of the day? Consider how close the car parking is and whether there is any point during the day when people need to move between buildings.

Snow and cold

If it is likely to be cold then you need to consider the impact on people's arrival time. Both delegates and speakers could encounter transport problems. As with wet weather, consider whether there is sufficient cloakroom space. A good system for handing over and retrieving coats can make all the difference to the smooth running of an event.

Sunshine

Hot weather can also cause transport problems — from overheating car engines through to a sudden surge of people heading for the beach! Sadly, your delegates might also decide to join the convoy to the coast, so you might need to prepare for a higher than average drop-out rate.

HEATING AND AIR CONDITIONING

Of course the weather outside the venue is only one part of the equation. You also need to consider the temperature indside. Unfortunately, what is a comfortable atmosphere for one person is often too cold for concentration or too warm for wakefulness for others. Even when the temperature seems fine at the beginning of the day, once a room is full of networking, active individuals things can heat up.

Check with the venue to find out how much control you have over the temperature — what are their heating and air conditioning arrangements? Preferably individual syndicate rooms have their own controls, so that workshop leaders, for instance, can check that delegates are happy with the temperature and can adapt as the day progresses.

If there isn't air conditioning, then find out whether or not windows can be opened without letting in too much noise. Also see if there are any fans available. Find out how individual radiators operate and make sure that whoever is working in the room knows how to change the temperature.

Artificial temperature control means that you might be able to make meetings fairly comfortable for the majority of delegates, but there are two drawbacks: noise and dryness. You will need to hear the noise level for yourself to decide whether or not it's acceptable. To combat dryness, you'll need to ensure there is a jug of water for speakers and delegates.

PRIZES AND MERCHANDISE

Many events include items available as prizes or for sale. Some of the issues to consider are:

- insurance — have you insured your goods against damage, theft and even against being won?
- security — who is going to look after the items throughout your event? Have you arranged cover for them so that they can take comfort breaks?
- receipts — are you issuing any kind of receipt as proof of purchase?
- storing money — where are you going to store the money that comes in? Who takes overall responsibility for it?
- stock control — how many items are you providing? Do you mind if they are all bought or won in the first half of the event or do you want to steadily bring out more items throughout the event? How are you keeping a record of items bought and items still in storage?
- change — people never have the correct money; how much of a cash float are you going to provide and in what denomination of notes and coins?
- bulk purchases — are there any discount arrangements for people buying more than one unit?
- pricing display — how are you indicating the price of an item? Are you going to arrange any point-of-sale promotional material?

You might also be providing free, branded merchandise (stickers, balloons, pens, etc). Some of the factors to consider with this sort of material are:

- appropriateness — how will the material go down with your delegates? Will they think it is fun and useful, or tacky and patronising?
- manufacture — where have your goods been made? (Check their origin to ensure there is no likelihood that manufacturers exploit child labour, for instance.) Are they made from recycled material? Can they be recycled?

General Principles and Issues

- cost — are you wasting money producing freebies or do they serve a valuable promotional purpose?

REFRESHMENTS AND SPECIAL DIETS

Refreshments

No matter how well organised your event, how stimulating the content and how exciting the outcomes, your delegates won't be satisfied if you don't give them biscuits with their coffee. This might be a slight exaggeration and it might just mean that your event was so good that the only thing they could think to put on their evaluation sheet was a criticism about the lack of jammy dodgers. But the point is that refreshments are an essential ingredient in most events.

The different types of refreshments an event organiser might have to arrange include the following.

1. Breakfast (for breakfast meetings/seminars and launches). People's tastes are very varied first thing in the morning, so try to provide as wide a choice as possible. Also try to provide healthy foods.
2. Teas/coffees (on arrival, mid-morning and mid-afternoon). Remember that not everyone drinks tea and coffee, and it's worth trying to establish this in advance so that you can lay on hot water, special herbal teas/infusions, decaffeinated drinks, etc. It can be quite hard to sort out an alternative if you only have a 15 minute break.
3. Lunch (from cold finger buffet to hot sit-down meal). *"A good tip for attracting black participants is the provision of hot food. Everyone likes food at events, but this is particularly so amongst African, African Caribbean, Asian and Chinese cultures. Go to any event organised by these communities and see the important role food plays. But there is no point*

providing food unless it is culturally appropriate," advises Sia's Barry Mussenden.

It is worth careful negotiation with the venue to get an appropriate menu at an affordable price and check the serving arrangements are acceptable.

4. Drinks reception (either as an event in its own right or as a pre-event welcome). Ensure you have sufficient soft drinks, and make sure you are not encouraging drink driving.
5. Dinner (again this could be an informal buffet or a sit-down meal). If you are organising a dinner then you might well have to co-ordinate a seating plan. Start work on this at the earliest opportunity and ensure there is a clear understanding over who has a say in the plan as this can become a tricky issue.

SPECIAL DIETS

If people have specific dietary requirements then it is important to accommodate them. Food can have particular religious, cultural, ethical, and health significance and you might need to liaise with individual delegates and your caterers to provide something appropriate.

Try to prompt delegates into being clear about what they can choose to eat by asking an open ended question and giving them space for details. *"Ask the question 'Do you have any specific dietary needs, eg vegetarian/halal?' In other words keep the question more open than a single vegetarian/non vegetarian box (but don't ask about halal meat if you are not going to provide it),"* says Sia's Barry Mussenden.

Some dietary issues to look out for are:

- vegetarian (and specific type, eg lacto vegetarian) — it is amazing how many caterers think that vegetarians eat fish, so you might need to check carefully with them. Also ask them to mark foods carefully so that vegetarians don't have to pick their way through the food to find out what is suitable

- gluten-free (no wheat products) — check with the delegate to see what they prefer to eat and liaise with the venue so that you know what they intend to provide. Check that this is acceptable to the delegate
- low-fat — again you will need to act as a go-between to find out what the delegate would like to eat and what the venue can provide in your budget range
- halal meat, as Sia points out, only specify this as an option if you are going to provide it
- no pork/beef (other meat types) — you might ask the delegate if they would prefer to select the vegetarian option. It's worth talking it through with them to find out what is appropriate
- no nut products — some people have potentially fatal nut allergies so it is vital that you give the caterers strict instructions and ensure that all foods are marked appropriately
- no tea/coffee — some people are able to drink decaffeinated products, herbal teas, etc. Others prefer hot water or a fruit juice alternative. Find out what is appropriate and ensure it is easily on-hand at the venue.

The key to specific dietary requirements is finding out:

- what the dietary requirement is exactly
- what the venue can provide
- whether what the venue is offering is appropriate
- whether there are any special arrangements on the day for the delegate to identify their refreshments (eg will it be held back behind the counter?)

GETTING PEOPLE TO THE EVENT

First you've got to get people to agree to attend, then you've actually got to get them to turn up. In this section we look at both of these areas.

AGREEMENT TO ATTEND

"Encourage people to book early to be sure of a place — devise incentives for early booking such as discount tickets, free lunch, group bookings and the like," says Artswork's Ruth Jones. Even if your event is free, you have to "sell" it to get people to put it in their diaries. You need to identify the benefits to your target audience and then spell them out.

Some of the messages you might include in an invitation or promotional material are:

- you have a need/problem (or ask the question — do you have a need/problem?), we have the answer or can help you find the solution
- our event is value for money/a bargain
- this is the only event of its kind you'll get the chance to attend in this area/this year
- anyone who's anybody will be there and you'll have lots of opportunity to network
- our event will be fun, you're guaranteed a good time
- there will be free/cheap food
- you will get some nice freebies
- you'll have an opportunity to make a valuable contribution
- you will go away with lots of new ideas and skills
- you can meet a celebrity/star attraction.

All of the above are hooks to attract people. They are the sorts of things you would also include in a news release when you are looking for media coverage.

If you are sending out written invites and asking people to respond, then make it as easy as possible. Include clear details of where to reply to. Enclose a tear off slip with plenty of room for people to fill in. Consider a reply-paid envelope or freepost address. Print a telephone number for further information. Allow for multiple bookings on the same reply slip.

TURNING UP

It's one thing getting people to say they will come to your event (even paying money for tickets), but it's another thing to actually get them there.

"To ensure people turn up, make sure you have sent confirmation of the booking, that they have the correct details and a decent map," advises Charlotte Macpherson of the NCVO. *"If you were concerned, you could do a phone around, but it is unlikely that close to the event you would have the time to do this. At any event you experience a drop-off rate on the day."*

No matter what you do people will always drop out at the last minute. There will be an emergency at the office, there will be a family problem, some people might simply forget to attend. On average you can expect a drop-out rate of between five and ten per cent.

Whether or not you want to take a risk and book proportionately less refreshments is up to you. If delegates have paid, it's probably better to err on the side of caution — at least there will be more food for everyone else.

There are some ways of keeping drop-out rates to a minimum:

- send people a reminder or further information shortly before the event (to jog their memories)
- have set cancellation charges or a strict no-refunds policy
- encourage people to send substitutes if they ring you up to cancel their place
- be flexible and allow people to attend for part of the event if another commitment comes up — let them dip in to those bits of the event that are most important to them
- continue to "sell" the event through media coverage, etc so that the event is high profile and seen as valuable for networking opportunities alone.

BRIEFINGS

Good communications are vital at every stage of event organisation and you will probably have regular meetings and briefings as things progress. A few days, or a week, before the event itself is a good time to issue some final briefing notes.

You will need to issue briefings to:

- staff and volunteers who are helping at the event
- speakers/workshop leaders
- sponsors/exhibitors
- the venue owners.

The most detailed briefings will be for helpers at the event. Try to include as much information as possible without overwhelming people. A typical briefing for staff and volunteers would include some background information, details of who is involved, roles and responsibilities, timings (from set-up to break-down), troubleshooting instructions, information about VIPs and venue contacts.

Speakers need less of a practical briefing (they should be confident that you have things under control) and instead need more of a reminder about audience, format and expected content. They do, though, need details of when to arrive, where to stay, how to get to the venue, a/v arrangements and details of any rehearsals. Sponsors/exhibitors need similar information to speakers. In addition they might want background information on speakers and delegates.

The key things to include in the briefing for the venue are:

- a reminder of your booking arrangements (all of the a/v equipment hired, refreshment details, rooms booked, etc). It is useful to set this down in writing once more
- details of the agenda, with emphasis on any short breaks where refreshments need to be served quickly and efficiently
- a reminder about arrangements for people with special diets

- details of any sub-contractors/exhibitors who will be delivering materials for the event
- contact details prior to the event and on the day
- delegate numbers
- wording for any signage at the venue.

SIGNPOSTING

The three types of signposting that you will need to consider are:

- signposts to the venue from surrounding roads/locations
- signage at the entrance to the venue to point people to the reception/registration area
- signage internally to help people find their way around.

EXTERNAL SIGNPOSTS

Many venues are clearly signposted from a couple of miles away — the venue itself will have made these arrangements to attract people to its location. Good maps and obvious road signs will enable people to find their way. You might want to organise additional signage (say, AA or RAC signs). It is a good way of raising the profile of your event in the neighbourhood and also to give it additional status.

Allow yourself a couple of months to get these signs organised as clearance needs to be obtained through the relevant local authority. Also, think of the snappy wording you want on the sign so that the information is obvious to participants but also clear to people who hadn't heard of the event before.

ENTRANCE SIGNAGE

Once people have arrived at your venue you need to consider how easy it is for them to find their way to the reception/registration area. It might be that the venue has a clearly marked main entrance and you are just inside the door. You might need to make your presence more obvious. Or, again, you might simply want to raise the profile through branding outside.

You can draw people's attention through banners, arrows, freestanding signs, exhibition panels and other devices at the entrance. Often delegates can feel a little uneasy when they arrive alone at an event. Branding at the entrance will give them confidence that they have come to the right place. It can be quite welcoming and also raises the sense of the importance of the event.

One final thing to remember about external branding is to make it weather proof.

INTERNAL SIGNAGE

Your delegates have found their way to the registration desk, but can they easily get to any other areas without getting lost or asking for help? A floorplan or map can help, but arrows, clearly marked doors, etc are extremely helpful. If you are going to put up signs inside a venue ensure the owners are happy with this and approve the blue-tac (for instance) that you are using to stick signs up. You will need to allow yourself at least an hour to put up signs and arrows (they only take about five minutes to take down at the end though!).

You might need to produce your signs or arrows on coloured paper or in a distinctive style to ensure they stand out from other material at the venue. Once you have put up your signs try to follow them yourself — or get someone else to try to follow them. Have some spare sheets and a marker pen available for any last minute signs you need to produce (or better still use a computer at the venue to produce higher quality signs).

CAR PARKING

Car parking is one of the issues to consider when booking a venue. It is good to encourage people to use public transport, but inevitably a high proportion of delegates will come by car.

Many venues have on-site car parking. This is great as long as this on-site car park has the capacity to cope with the number of cars that your event could generate. It is worth asking the question, finding out if a specific area can be reserved and discovering what back-up arrangements there are. Always explain the car parking arrangements clearly to delegates and others involved in your event so they allow sufficient time to arrive and bring money, if necessary, for parking.

If there isn't a free on-site car park then you will need to look at what is available nearby. There might be private multi-storey car parks or long-term public car parks. Mark various alternatives on your maps to the venue and explain the likely cost. Also, find out if there is a park and ride option as this can be far cheaper.

Be clear about parking provision for orange badge holders and, if necessary, reserve some spaces. If you have reserved any parking spaces you will need to ensure these are clearly marked and that someone is on hand to move cones for the appropriate guests.

TOILETS

Toilet facilities are essential. If you are holding an event out of doors then you might well need to organise some portable loos if there aren't

Organising Effective Events

facilities nearby. Even when there are toilets available you need to consider a number of issues.

First, how many toilets are there and are there enough for the number of people you are expecting to come to your event? (Remember to find out if other people will also be using them during the day.) Also it is well worth going into the toilets yourself when you are researching your venue. Don't just note them down on your floorplan, take a look inside to see what they are like. Find out how often they are serviced and what you will need to do if paper towels, toilet rolls, etc run out. As discussed above, check the accessibility and number of toilets for disabled people.

Think about where the toilets are in relation to your event and how much time you have allowed for comfort breaks. Mark the toilets clearly on any delegate literature and ensure they are signposted clearly within the venue itself.

FIRST AID

First aid arrangements will seem more or less important depending on the nature of your event (from society lunch to bungee jump). However, you always need to have first aid facilities on hand.

In some cases you will need the support of an organisation like St John Ambulance. At other events it will be more appropriate to have a qualified first aider in attendance (either the venue's own or a member of your team). Make sure they know where the venue's first aid box is. It might also be worth checking that the first aid box has been replenished.

General Principles and Issues

REGISTRATION/BADGING

It is important to find out how many people come to your event and, if possible, who they are. If you are asking people to book places in advance then you will already have a good idea. If people can just turn up on the day then you will need to try to capture as much information as possible.

REGISTRATION

Registration on arrival is the standard way of recording who attends your event. Many venues need to know this information in case there is a fire or some other reason for an emergency evacuation. If people have booked in advance then you can produce a registration list. People simply tick themselves in and this saves lots of time. Produce the list in alphabetical order — either according to surname or by organisation. If you are asking people to sign themselves in giving their name and organisation, then you might want to have a number of registration points/books available to speed things up. Ask for a telephone number, if not a full address, so that you can stay in touch with delegates and give them information about future events. Better still, ask for business cards if they have them — this will really speed up the registration process whilst giving you their contact details.

BADGING

Badging is another consideration. Networking is such a valuable part of any event and people need to know who they are talking with. You can produce a variety of different types of badges. You can buy badge-making machines. You can run off labels through a computer and mount these on card. You can hand write names onto sticky labels.

Badges provide another branding opportunity and you can add a small logo to most badges that run through a laser printer. Before deciding on the appropriate type of badge, it's worth considering what people will want to wear at the event. Badging won't be in keeping with a formal dinner, for instance. Would people prefer clip-on or pin badges?

If participants are wearing badges, you should consider asking them to remove the badges before photographs are taken. If your speakers are wearing badges ask them to take them off before they go on stage — badges look scrappy on photos and videos.

WHAT TO WEAR

What you wear at your event is, of course, up to you. Your clothes are a matter of personal choice and reflect your personality, to a degree. At the same time, though, you need to think about the impression they convey — particularly if you are representing an organisation.

If there is time for you to get changed during the day, then it's worth wearing comfortable casual clothes while you are setting up, and then smarter clothes for the event itself. Your outfit for the event still needs to be comfortable — perhaps with layers so that you can strip off as things hot up during the day. Try to keep your clothes simple too, particularly if you are going to be on stage or in any photographs. Don't forget to think carefully about appropriate, comfortable shoes.

ON-THE-DAY COMMUNICATIONS

"The co-ordinator must have absolutely no designated tasks on the day so that they can either spend the time smiling serenely whilst everything runs

General Principles and Issues

smoothly, or running round in a mad panic covering everything that has been forgotten, coping with unexpected emergencies or taking over from people who haven't turned up," suggests Artswork's Ruth Jones.

Whether you are happily watching everything come together on the day or dashing about troubleshooting you will have plenty of communicating to do. You could be running through checklists, welcoming speakers, pointing delegates in the right direction, chasing up a/v equipment. At the same time you will be liaising with your support team and the venue.

To ensure this communication is swift and effective you could:

- use mobile phones or walkie talkies so that you can keep in constant contact
- issue everyone with a detailed timetable so that they know where key people are if they need to liaise with them
- make use of the venue's tannoy system
- schedule in on-the-day briefings, etc
- ensure you have runners to fetch people
- use a message board — for both organisers and participants.

When problems arise don't look to blame someone for letting you down, concentrate on finding a solution — you can hold a post mortem later if appropriate. When things go well give instant feedback and praise.

CHECKLISTS

Your initial event plan will probably provide you with a good working checklist. It is worth revisiting this nearer to the event in case things have been added or changed. Checklists can be very reassuring for the event organiser and can help to reduce your stress levels. It can also be very constructive for the whole event team to be involved in compiling and running through a checklist.

Organising Effective Events

Below is a sample checklist which you can add to or subtract from as appropriate. It is not a timetable — some things will go on simultaneously and different things can happen at different times.

1. Venue
Draw up venue criteria
Shortlist possible venues
Visit venues
Select venue
Confirm booking requirements and price with venue
Confirm car parking arrangements

2. Format
Agree agenda for event
Prepare briefing notes for speakers, etc
Book speakers, etc
Copywrite invitations, promotional material, delegate packs, etc
Devise evaluations

3. Budget
Draw up budget
Secure additional funding if needed
Sign agreement with funder
Agree pricing

4. Date
Agree date
Book venue for the date
Book speakers/workshop leaders for the date, issue contracts if appropriate

5. Print
Produce invitations, flyers, posters and other promotional material
Produce delegate packs, agendas, floorplans, evaluations, brochures, menus, trainers' notes, on-the-day material
Photocopy material

Produce badges

6. Promotional
Organise mailings
Send news releases
Other promotional activity (adverts, etc)

7. Audio visual
Confirm a/v requirements with speakers
Book a/v equipment and write confirmation letter
Confirm power points at venue
Agree set and staging requirements

8. Team
Agree roles and responsibilities
Hold team briefings
Organise travel and overnights
Arrange petty cash

9. Response mechanism
Process replies to invitations
Send joining instructions
Find out any access, dietary, communication needs and make arrangements
Confirm arrangements with relevant participants

10. Refreshments
Confirm numbers
Confirm special dietary requirements
Confirm menu for refreshment breaks and timings

11. Other
Agree first aid and health and safety arrangements
Confirm security instructions
Notify insurers

EVALUATION

You will have a good feel for how the event has gone, but independent feedback from delegates, speakers and everyone else who has been involved is invaluable. Evaluations can help to motivate you and your team (when you hear how much people have enjoyed your event and how helpful it has been for them). Delegate feedback will help you to improve similar events in the future. It is very helpful as you discuss the event with any funders involved.

Feedback from speakers/participants is also very valuable. They might suggest ways you could improve your briefing process or a/v support, for instance. The views of sponsors should also be sought, because the event has to work for them too. Feedback from sponsors will probably be through discussion or a letter, but feedback from speakers and delegates should be through a formal questionnaire.

When you are designing an evaluation form for delegates and speakers these are some of the things to consider:

- try to keep the evaluation to a maximum of two sides of A4, one side is preferable
- use multiple choice options where possible, but also leave space for comments
- when using a scale of numbers to rate satisfaction, go for 1 to 8, or 1 to 6 rather than 1 to 10 as it prompts clarity
- ask for views on both format and content of the event
- ask for views about the venue (the venue might appreciate the feedback and it will help you to decide whether or not to return on future occasions)
- leave a space for further remarks at the end of the questionnaire
- ask people to return their forms before they depart
- use the evaluation as a market research opportunity — ask about other similar events that delegates might attend.

SPECIFIC EVENTS

Most of the general principles outlined in the first section of this book apply to all events. However, there are some specific additional issues that are worth considering with particular types of events as well as the tricks and traps to watch out for.

ANNUAL GENERAL MEETINGS

For many small charities an annual general meeting (AGM) is a quick and fairly low-key affair. This reflects the limited sums of time and money available

However, an AGM can also be an opportunity to reward and motivate staff and volunteers (by telling them how successful they have been). At the same time it gives you an occasion to invite funders and potential funders. You can show them your achievements and what you hope to do in the coming year. There is also an opportunity to reach a wider audience of VIPs and the local community through your AGM.

FOCUSING THE EVENT

You don't want to bore people though. You might want to run through previous minutes and some of the detailed financial reports with relevant trustees and committees before inviting a wider audience to a presentation and refreshments.

WHERE TO HOLD YOUR AGM

If your organisation has more than one site then you will need to decide on an appropriate location for the event. This may or may not be at your own premises.

WHEN TO HOLD YOUR AGM

Another major consideration is when to hold such an event — over lunch or in the early evening tend to be the best times.

THE TONE OF THE EVENT

Finally, you will need to think about the overall tone of the event. If you are really upbeat and provide a sumptuous spread of food then people might think you are obviously rolling in money. If you go for a meagre buffet and moan about your stretched circumstances people might think you are unprofessional and unable to manage your resources. You probably need to strike a balance — conveying a professional, caring and efficient image. You will achieve this with strong displays and presentations, decent food, and by outlining a vision for the future if additional funding is available.

AUCTIONS

Auctions are quite specialised events and it is worth involving someone who has experience of them. Auctions don't have to take place in a venue at all. They can be conducted over the radio, through the Internet or through sealed written bids, for instance. The most common auctions still involve an auctioneer and bidders meeting up in the same room (even if one or two bidders participate via phone lines).

If you have some stunning things on offer and you want national, if not global, offers then you will probably work through a professional auction house. However, the concern here is with smaller scale auctions organised at a local level.

THEMED AUCTIONS

You might want to set a theme for the auction before you invite donations from individuals and organisations. This helps you to focus the event and will give people an idea of what they can contribute. It gives a good news angle too for you to use in your promotional material.

PRICING AND AUCTIONEER

You will need to set a policy on starting prices and reserve prices (below which you are not prepared to sell the item). You will also need a charismatic auctioneer. The personality of the auctioneer has a huge influence on the success of an auction. They can help to sell the items through their descriptions of them, and they can identify likely buyers and encourage them to bid against one another. Auctions should be fun too, so your auctioneer needs a good sense of humour. However, you shouldn't miss the opportunity to give your organisation, cause and campaigns a plug — through an opening address and literature at the event.

AUCTIONING PROMISES

Auctions don't have to feature tangible products — why not consider an "auction of promises"? These events feature gifts in kind of a wide variety of services. They can range from an offer to mow your lawn (by an individual) through to the servicing of your car (by a garage) or drafting of your will (by a firm of solicitors).

CUSTOMER SATISFACTION

The other main issue to consider is customer satisfaction. What happens if there is a problem with one of the items you sell? Or, if you are running an auction of promises, what happens if the offer of a service never materialises or is sub-standard? You need to know where you stand on such legal issues and have relevant insurance in place.

BALLS, DINNERS AND THEMED EVENINGS

Such occasions are normally glamorous, high profile and expensive (both to organise and, usually, to attend).

BUDGET CAREFULLY

Because these events are costly they have to be budgeted thoroughly to ensure the income is going to be sufficient (whether from sponsors or individual ticket sales). Don't budget so tightly that you have to sell every single seat at every table — your own team will need to be accommodated. Be prepared for several last minute bookings too. If you have sold a table to a group of VIPs you don't want to turn any of their extra guests away.

MENUS

It's never easy to select menus for other people. However, you will need to limit people's choice so that the kitchen and waiting staff can cope. As long as you clearly inform people before the event as to what the menu is then they have ample opportunity to let you know if they need an alternative.

Take advice on your choice of foods, particularly if you are targeting a wide cross-section of the community. Consider how the whole menu hangs together rather than plumping for appetising sounding individual courses. If possible, sample some of the food you have chosen.

DRINKS

Guests need to be clear about whether or not any alcoholic or soft drinks are being provided with the meal. They might need to book and buy bottles of wine in advance, for instance. Or you could ask them to pay for after dinner liqueurs separately. If drinks aren't going to flow for free then guests will need to bring money with them, so they need to know in advance.

Encourage guests to travel by taxi if they are going to have a drink — make it easy for them to book cabs at the end of the evening by alerting local taxi companies.

ENTERTAINMENT

Are you having music and entertainment at your evening event? If so, how are you booking your entertainers? Many venues can put you in touch with appropriate entertainers or will book them for you. The advantage to this is that the venue will use people they know and rely on — you are guaranteed a certain quality and it is easy to make the arrangements.

If, though, you want to bring in other entertainers who are new to the venue then you will need to discuss with them:

- setting up time
- rehearsal time
- power points (if needed) and any p/a equipment required
- fees (specifying the times they are required)
- cancellation charges
- appropriate dress.

You will need to brief entertainers about the nature and tone of your event. You might need to give them details about particular people who will be attending.

SMOKING

Many dinners are non-smoking until coffee is served and all of the speeches have been made. You will need to set a clear policy and accommodate people who want to be in a non-smoking area.

TABLE PLANS

Drawing up a table plan ensures all your guests are seated fairly quickly and easily on the night. However, it's not an easy task to compile the

Specific Events

plan. Be prepared for lots of juggling as the event gets nearer and have a clear rationale as to why certain people should be seated with others.

BRANDING

There are other branding opportunities in addition to the invitations and delegate material. You might want to hang banners or have a display at the event. You might want the menus and table cards to carry your branding. You might want to have branded wine bottles. Think about the different messages you want to get across and take advantage of the various spaces and printed materials that will be available on the night.

If your event is a straightforward fundraising ball with an after dinner speaker, take the opportunity to promote your organisation. You can do this with a quick welcome at the top of the evening or as you introduce or thank the speaker. Keep any plug of this kind short and punchy, and as lighthearted as possible. Use the event as a networking opportunity and then follow up with the harder edged fundraising appeal afterwards.

CONFERENCES

Organising a conference is always a massive task, and stuff-to-do lists are essential (and usually very long!). Attention to detail is absolutely vital and all of the considerations covered in the first half of this pocketbook are relevant. Some specific things to look out for include: programming, scheduling and briefing speakers, incorporating question times, co-ordinating delegates and post-conference reports.

PROGRAMMING

The decision to organise a conference often grows out of another project. A conference is a way to spread good practice, seek views and share ideas. It might be used to kick start a consultation process, to review progress to date, or to disseminate lessons learned. A conference is usually a means to an end rather than an end in itself — and so the broad themes and content are already decided on.

Even so, you will still need to give careful consideration to the detailed programming. It's difficult to do this alone and a small brainstorming committee is often helpful. Try not to overfill the day, but on the other hand don't cover issues for the sake of filling up slots. Your plenary sessions and any workshops should be firmly focused on achieving outcomes that fit with your conference's aims and objectives.

SCHEDULING AND BRIEFING SPEAKERS

When allocating slots to speakers remember that "less is more". The ideal conference speech is no more than 20 minutes in length (and often only 10), with time for questions. A short slot keeps the speaker focused and punchy, and retains the audience's interest.

Give speakers as much information as possible about the aims and objectives of the conference, the context of their slot and the issues to be covered by other speakers. This will help to prevent duplications and irrelevance. You might want to meet up with speakers in advance to discuss their contribution. However, this won't always be appropriate and you will need to judge whether or not the speaker will find this helpful.

Specific Events

INCORPORATING QUESTION TIMES

Audience interaction is important, so allow time in your schedule for questions. Some conference organisers allocate question time after each individual speaker. Others run up to three speakers back to back before a panel question and answer session. Both approaches work equally well.

CO-ORDINATING DELEGATES

Co-ordinating speakers is one thing, shepherding delegates is quite another. Often you will need to move over 100 people between various rooms — even if it's just for refreshments. It's worth having a pre-arranged system. This could involve working with a couple of people to "spread the word" amongst delegates that it's time to move between rooms, it might mean setting up a separate microphone in the refreshment area, it could involve a megaphone, or it might mean making use of the venue's public address system.

Allow yourself time to move people between sessions or refreshment breaks, and start to move them five minutes before you want the next session to begin. Lots of people wait until this final moment before nipping off to the toilet! Remember to round up the smokers who could be lurking outside the main entrance.

POST CONFERENCE REPORTS

Many people like to have copies of speakers' notes or entire speeches. You might need to record the speeches to allow transcripts to be produced. You might have to organise notetakers or rapporteurs to sit in on any workshops. Be clear of what's required in advance to make things as easy as possible.

EXHIBITIONS, ROADSHOWS AND DISPLAYS

This section examines some of the issues relating to exhibitions, roadshows and displays; in particular: exhibition space, attracting attention, give-aways and privacy.

EXHIBITION SPACE

If you are running a roadshow and taking your exhibition into a public area then you need to have a clear and detailed agreement with the site owner. Ensure you know the precise dimensions of the area allocated to your display — and this includes the height. Also find out how many power points are nearby and whether or not you are free to use them (don't forget to bring along gaffer tape to secure any wires and extension leads).

If you are organising an exhibition — either as a stand-alone event or as part of a larger conference — then you will need to give out very detailed information to each exhibitor. You might also need to have an agreement with several contractors so that exhibitors can buy in extras directly from them. Usually these extras will include: lights and other electrical items, flowers, cleaning services, security and "shell schemes" (on which they build their displays).

You will need to give clear dimensions (including available height). Setting up and breaking down directions need to be detailed and stringent (otherwise people will arrive late and will try to take down their display whilst people are still visiting the exhibition). Exhibitors will need to be clearly badged to distinguish them from visitors. You will have to ensure there are adequate refreshments and toilet facilities available.

ATTRACTING ATTENTION

If you are the exhibitor then your display will be designed to attract attention, but there are additional things you can do to entice people to your stand or roadshow.

The first thing is to publicise your attendance at the event — through local press and radio (either editorial or advertising). If you are going for editorial then there will have to be something newsworthy about your exhibition — perhaps it is the first of its kind, maybe you will be giving out astonishing information, or maybe people will have the chance to win an interesting prize.

Another technique is the production of flyers to be distributed to people who are passing nearby. If you can offer an opportunity to win a prize or something tempting then they might pay a visit to your stand to find out more. Sandwich boards or "ice cream" stands are similar to flyers. They draw in passing crowds. You could also use sound to attract attention — music or announcements — but check with the venue first to ensure that this is acceptable (particularly if it is a residential area).

GIVE-AWAYS

Have plenty of things to hand out to people who visit your exhibition or roadshow. Even small stickers and balloons go down well. Ensure you have sufficient stocks of information leaflets and business cards too. Bags and mugs are popular forms of merchandise and you can use them to get across your brand with a memorable message. Once other people see their friends with these gifts they will be attracted to your stand.

Organising Effective Events

PRIVACY

One final thing to consider either when you are exhibiting or hosting an exhibition is privacy. You might need to ask for a room to be made available nearby or build in a screened-off section to your exhibition so that visitors can discuss sensitive matters in confidence.

FAIRS AND FÊTES

Fairs and fêtes are often annual events with one individual, or a committee, taking responsibility year after year. It is important that they document the processes involved so that others can support them and take over easily when the time comes.

Particular issues connected with fairs and fêtes are: motivating participants, location, involving local businesses and novelties.

MOTIVATING PARTICIPANTS

Fairs and fêtes depend on many people giving up their time to prepare, set up and be involved on the day. Successful fêtes rely on motivated stallholders. As in any activity, motivation depends on:

- clear briefing and expectations
- balancing responsibility with the authority to make decisions
- gratitude expressed for every aspect of their contribution
- identification with the aims and objectives.

LOCATION

The location of your fête might not be an issue because it always takes place in the same garden or field. However, if you are deciding on a new location, then the following things need to be considered:

- powerpoints and extension leads
- hot and cold running water
- toilet facilities
- health and safety (particularly of children), ie is there a river or pond nearby?
- parking facilities.

INVOLVING LOCAL BUSINESSES

Another thing to consider is how you can involve local businesses in your fête. Many local businesses like to get involved in fêtes because it means just a once a year commitment, they are guaranteed a good audience, and they are clearly linking up with the local community. You might be able to ask them for:

- items or services to give as prizes in a raffle/draw
- sponsorship of a specific stall or activity
- provision of an attraction (eg bouncy castle, balloon ride, etc as relevant).

NOVELTIES

As fêtes happen each year you are guaranteed a certain level of success thanks to your loyal supporters. However, it's worth brainstorming each year to see if you can come up with a winning novelty to bring in extra visitors. This could be anything from a raffled ride in a rally car through to a line dancing marathon.

FESTIVALS

Festivals celebrate culture, community and talent. This section looks at programming, inclusiveness and spin-offs.

PROGRAMMING

Programming is at the heart of festival organisation. It's a tough process and you need to take care not to raise people's expectations before booking them to take part. Brainstorming with others is again crucial. Find out what's worked in festivals elsewhere and, if there are touring groups that can get involved in your festival, consider involving them.

There might be local expertise on hand too. Talk to your local council — they might have an arts officer or community development specialist who can assist you with your planning.

INCLUSIVENESS

Festivals usually have a particular focus — on an art form (eg jazz), a theme (eg folk arts, crafts, dance and music) or a geographical area. But they should be inclusive — involving all elements of the community. You might need to liaise with a range of professionals to ensure you involve all ages, cultures, etc.

Truly successful festivals bring different groups together to celebrate a common issue or interest. They provide an opportunity for people to learn from one another and get to know each other through this shared focus. It's a shame to miss this opportunity because it's easier to rely on a group of committed individuals.

SPIN-OFFS

When you are planning your festival you need to consider the range of spin-off benefits — they can help you attract sponsorship and win the commitment of local people to the project. Spin-offs include:

- increased trade for local shops, hotels, transport and entertainments
- raised profile of your organisation, even amongst those who don't attend — showing you to be vibrant and forward-looking
- improved sense of community, involvement and networking.

FUNDRAISING SPECIAL EVENTS

Special events to raise funds for your organisation can take very many different forms. They can't all be covered here, but there are some general reminders that apply to all such events. These include: putting things in writing, staying within the law, health and safety, fun fundraising and security.

PUTTING THINGS IN WRITING

Charity law demands that everything to do with fundraising must be stated clearly in writing. However, it's important to do more than meeting your legal requirements. Some of the things participants need or usually want to know include:

- the proportion of funds raised going directly to help others
- exactly what they are doing, what is expected of them and when
- where to send any monies raised and in what form
- how to publicise what they're doing

STAYING WITHIN THE LAW

There are lots of rules surrounding fundraising and it's important to keep within the law. It's important to check the latest legal developments to ensure your event meets all of the necessary requirements.

HEALTH AND SAFETY

When you are thinking about the various legal issues relating to fundraising don't forget broader health and safety considerations. It's all very well to think that sitting in a bath of beans will be a great money-spinner — but is it safe and hygienic? If in doubt, ask your local environmental health officer for advice.

FUN FUNDRAISING

Fundraising should emphasise fun. The more enjoyable the experience is, the greater the effort and commitment of participants and the bigger the funds will be.

SECURITY

If money is going to be donated at a specific site then you need to consider how it is stored securely and how it will be transported to the bank. If you are holding your event in the evening or at the weekend then you might need to make arrangements in advance for the storage of money until the banks re-open.

OPEN DAYS

Words can't always convey just what your organisation does. Sometimes people need to experience your work in action — and that might mean coming to your centre or place of work. You can invite people along on an ad hoc basis, but many organisations find it worthwhile to set up a special open day.

CONSULTING STAFF/USERS

If you are going to throw open your doors you need to be sure that everyone is comfortable with the idea, including staff, volunteers and users of your services. You need to involve all of your constituents in planning the event, and it helps if they are given a range of roles on the day too. If you don't involve everyone in this way then your open day is in danger of resembling a visit to the zoo.

WHO TO INVITE

Your guest list will reflect the purpose of your event. If you are holding your open day to show neighbouring residents what you do, then they will form the bulk of your guest list. Equally, if you are encouraging supporters to donate additional monies, then you will focus on your existing funders.

Don't miss the opportunity to widen the event out and reach new audiences. Think ahead — are you going to open a new centre in another area? If you are, why not invite local residents along to find out more about what you do?

WHAT TO LAY ON

At its simplest, an open day can be just that — a normal day with completely open access to outside visitors. But it's probably better to welcome visitors with one or two extras — refreshments, a guided tour, a talk, literature about your work, a gift.

HOW TO CO-ORDINATE VISITORS

You might invite visitors to come along in groups at particular times of the day, focus the event around a couple of hours in the middle of the day, or have open house throughout the entire day. It's up to you and what you think will work best for your situation.

However, you will need a plan to co-ordinate visitors once they arrive. You will probably want them to sign in and out so that you know who is on your premises. You might want to give them a badge so that you can see who they are at a glance and also to encourage networking. You will need people to show them around, tell them more about your work and generally make their visit worthwhile. That means having a number of guides on hand throughout the event.

Don't forget to put up signs/arrows so that people can find their way around. You might need to give them a floorplan to help them. You might want them to leave their business card so that you can get in touch with them in the future. You could consider a prize draw to encourage people to leave their details. It's also worth asking people what they think of your organisation and its work — through an anonymous questionnaire as they leave. You might even ask them what they thought of you before the event and what they have learnt from their visit.

Specific Events

OPENINGS AND LAUNCHES

If you are opening a new centre or launching a new service then you might want to organise an event to mark the occasion. Issues to consider include: interested parties, ceremony/speeches and publicity.

INTERESTED PARTIES

As with a more general open day, it's worth thinking laterally and brainstorming your guest list so that you make the event as worthwhile as possible. You might not think that your local MP is particularly important to you now, but you could need their help in the future — so invite him or her along to show how valuable your work is.

Neighbouring residents might not have said much about your organisation or the impact you have locally, but they might be concerned about new developments in the future. Invite them along and show them what you do — get them involved and develop their understanding.

Your clients, customers or users need to know more about your work. If your new premises or services are to be a success they need to welcome them. If your services are sensitive and confidential then clients might not feel comfortable in attending a big launch event. As a result you might want to hold more than one launch event — one for clients and another for funders, etc. You might want to invite past clients who are happy to participate in an event, with another form of promotion to potential clients.

The local media will always be worth inviting (even though they rarely attend!) but it gives you an opportunity to get to know relevant journalists and to tell them more about your work in an informal conversation.

CEREMONIES/SPEECHES

You will usually want to incorporate some marker to make the opening "official". Exactly what you do will depend on your work and the setting. A straightforward speech, the cutting of a ribbon, a short performance, the unveiling of a plaque can all be appropriate. Take a photo to record the moment and use this in your media relations.

PUBLICITY

The local media may or may not come along to your opening — depending on how newsworthy they view it and what else is on their desk that particular day. So ensure you take your own photographs in case you need to issue them after the event.

You might think about the publicity angle when planning your event and decide to incorporate an interesting photo opportunity, or to invite a relevant famous person to add to the news interest of your opening. If no journalists attend the event, all is not lost. You might find some interesting additional angle on the day yourself — for instance an interesting or controversial remark made by your chairperson.

PROTESTS, DEMONSTRATIONS AND VIGILS

The issues involved in organising protests, demonstrations and vigils are slightly different to normal. They rarely involve booking a venue, for instance, but still require meticulous planning and professional organisation.

KEEPING WITHIN THE LAW

There are a number of laws and bylaws relating to protests and demonstrations — particularly on the numbers of people who can gather, where you can legally meet and where you can march. It is worth consulting your own organisation's solicitors and the relevant local authority to find out what you can do legitimately.

Once you have found out what is permissible, you might decide that your point can't be made effectively within the law. Before taking this step consider what can be done legally. Find out if your local council would be sympathetic to your need being heard — it might make arrangements for a legal demonstration. If your protest is going to be breaking any laws you must let all your invited participants know this and you must consult senior management and trustees to see if they agree with your actions.

In the end you might decide that an illegal demonstration could damage your charity's reputation and choose an alternative method instead. This might mean that you hold a public meeting rather than a march. It could mean a leaflet drop rather than a demonstration with placards. It could involve a staged photo opportunity instead of a blockade.

The key thing is to consider the purpose of the demonstration and then to ask whether you can achieve this in any other way.

PLACARDS AND BANNERS

A legal demonstration, protest or vigil can show effectively just how strongly people feel about an issue. The sheer number of people who turn out is one way of showing strength of feeling, but the messages on placards and banners are equally important.

The messages that come across need to be coherent. You might like to suggest the general text for placards and banners so that you are all saying something similar. Don't go for mass-produced placards or it will look as if the crowd is being manipulated by one or two people.

HEALTH AND SAFETY

If you are organising an all-night vigil, a march of any distance, or any activity that involves a crowd of people grouping together then you need to consider health and safety. You might need to involve an organisation such as the St John Ambulance or Red Cross so that trained first aiders are on hand. Ask them for further advice on what might be needed.

PRESS CONFERENCES AND PHOTO OPPORTUNITIES

The press spends little on staff photographers, radio journalists are scurrying all over the place and television crews are few and far between. However, they do attend a limited number of press conferences/photo opportunities. Don't expect more than a handful unless you are dealing with a major breaking national story and be prepared for no journalists at all!

You can still make such events worthwhile if you co-ordinate your own photographs and arrange down-the-line interviews. These are considered in more detail below, along with timing, choice of venue and media liaision.

TIMING

Press conferences and photo opportunities are best held in the morning — either first thing (with breakfast) or mid-morning (with coffee). You will need to give the journalists plenty of warning so that they can book it into the news diary and head off for your venue before they go into their offices. It's worth a quick courtesy call the previous day to see if they are intending to come along. If your press conference is being held to respond to a major crisis then the sooner the better. Journalists will be eager to attend, so the time of day won't be a problem.

CHOICE OF VENUE

As you are unlikely to be dealing with more than a handful of journalists, there's no need to book an expensive hall. Your own premises may be fine — particularly if you want to familiarise journalists with your work. The key things to consider when deciding on the venue for your press conference are:

- confidentiality — appropriate areas for interviews
- sound-proofing/quiet/appropriate background noise — for radio interviews
- background — logos and examples of your work for photo opportunities
- convenience — a central location that's easy for your target media to get to.

MEDIA LIAISON

There's a balance to be struck between leaving things to chance and annoying journalists. It's probably worth sending them details of your news conference/photo opportunity and then following up with one phone call to find out if they're intending to come along. It's up to them and if they decline, then you just have to accept it (and make the event more attractive next time).

If the journalist is unable to attend, send them a news release and, if appropriate, a photo after the event. Journalists are busy people and if they don't have to attend an event they won't. You should have something additional to the news release that makes it worth their while — the opportunity for interviews with key people, for instance, or the chance to report on a project in action.

PHOTOGRAPHERS

Increasingly newspapers are dependent on freelance photographers and contributions from the public. Find out who your target publications use frequently (look for the credit with the photo) and invite them along to your event. In some cases you will need to pay the freelance to attend. In other instances they might think it is worth their while because they'll be able to sell the picture on to the relevant publications. Take your own photos too and send in appropriate ones, clearly labelled and captioned.

Consider what props and logos you can make use of in the background to the photograph, to reinforce any messages you want to get across about your organisation.

DOWN-THE-LINE INTERVIEWS

The final issue to consider with a press conference is arrangements for down-the-line interviews. You may know in advance of the need to set something up, or a journalist who was intending to come along might not be able to make it, but still wants the interview. You don't need to set up anything too sophisticated, but you will need a quiet room with a phone line. You'll need to be clear about arrangements for ringing into the relevant radio station (ask who is going to make the call, at what time, and whether it will be live or recorded).

SEMINARS, WORKSHOPS AND TRAINING DAYS

The most important issues to consider when organising seminars, workshops and training days are the structure of the event, delegate participation, trainer liaison and the eventual outcomes.

STRUCTURE

Workshops, training days and seminars involve the participants in a lot of concentration and work. They mean time away from the workplace so that people are determined to get full value from such events. Therefore they have to be carefully structured — to pack in as much as possible without overtiring the delegates.

Some of the responsibility lies with the trainers or workshop leaders, but a lot depends on the structure of the event imposed by the organiser. Key points to consider include:

- the need for networking — allowing enough times in the breaks for chatting as well as refreshments
- mixing plenary and workshop sessions — so that there are some opportunities to relax and listen to others as well as getting stuck in
- the football match rule — never going for longer than 90 minutes without a break
- housekeeping — allowing time to explain the layout of the venue and the content of the day so that participants are clear about what they're doing, where and when.

PARTICIPATION

Learning through doing is an important aspect of any training day. Delegates should be encouraged to participate and you should let them know their likely degree of involvement before the event. It is important that your trainers and workshop leaders follow through on such promises and don't just deliver a lecture if you've promised role play and active learning.

TRAINER LIAISON

Every trainer has an individual style and specific techniques. However, you can give them a clear brief for their workshop, covering:

- aims and objectives
- subject matter to cover
- outcomes desired
- suggestions for practical activities.

Also give them details on the timings of their workshop, any background about delegates' skills, expectations and needs, and information about other workshops' content. After the event, feedback your views and any relevant delegate evaluation details.

OUTCOMES

Before your workshop you will have set yourself anticipated outcomes. The day might be thoroughly enjoyable and the feedback positive, but how do you know what the short-, medium- and long-term outcomes are? Delegate evaluation will give you some information, but you might need to set up a monitoring and reporting mechanism to keep informed.

AND FINALLY, ...

Event organisation is time consuming, exhausting, but ultimately very rewarding — both in terms of individual satisfaction and outcomes for your organisation, local community and all of those involved.

If you are to be a successful event organiser, you need to be like the careful driver who anticipates that everyone else on the road is about to make a mistake — assume that if anyone can let you down, they will. You must do more than this though — have a Plan B and Plan C to deal with all problems.

For example, if you book equipment, assume:

- it won't turn up on time
- it won't work properly, and
- it will break down in the middle of the event.

As a result, don't just worry, you should:

- build in extra setting up time and book the equipment before it is really needed
- ensure a technician sets the equipment up and shows key people how it works, and
- ensure a technician is on standby or is present at the event to put any faulty equipment right immediately. Build a clause into the

Organising Effective Events

booking of the equipment that allows for a reduced fee if there are any problems!

What else do you need to do apart from anticipating every possible problem or challenge? You need to:

- plan and prepare meticulously as far in advance as possible
- involve as many people as possible in brainstorming at every opportunity
- work to checklists and make them "living" or "evolving" documents that change over time
- consider equal opportunities in-depth and consult relevant organisations
- be prepared to delegate and be able to involve as many helpers as possible
- produce clear briefs for all speakers, participants, organisers, etc involved
- consider things from a delegate's point of view
- learn from others
- motivate those involved and deal diplomatically with difficulties
- evaluate what works and what doesn't — dispassionately
- have lots of support from friends, family and colleagues.

It's tough, but all events have an effect of some sort — from developing new skills to raising awareness of particular issues. You, the event organiser, can help to change people's lives and that's got to be worth the effort.

INDEX

A

access issues 12, 25, 33
advance bookings 15
advertising 18–19, 81
agenda details 60
agreement to attend 58
air conditioning 53
aisle space 31
announcements 81
annual events 11
annual general meetings 11, 71–2
Artswork 1, 7, 14, 16, 43, 58, 67
attention, attracting 81
attention to detail 1
attire, suitable 66
auctions 73–4
audience 4, 5–6
    see also target audience
audio visual and set 23, 25, 43–8, 69
    aids 44
    exhibition boards/set and staging 47–8
    lighting 47
    microphones and P/A system 43–4
    overhead projectors 44–5
    slide projector/computer screens 45–6
    video equipment 46
availability of event 6
awareness raising 4

B

backgrounds 93
badging 65–6, 80, 88
balls 74–7
banners 91–2
bathrooms 33
bedrooms 33
black and ethnic communities 6, 8, 55–6

black voluntary organisations 17
booking arrangements 14, 15, 58, 60, 97–8
Braille 51
brainstorming 3, 11, 83, 84, 89, 98
branding 10–13, 54, 62, 66, 77
breakfasts 50, 55
briefings 60–1, 67, 78
briefs 41, 98
British Association of Conference Towns 24
British Council of Organisations of Disabled People 27, 32, 33, 37, 38
British Sign Language 34
budgeting and pricing 11–13, 51, 68, 74–5
buffets 32
bulk purchases 54
business cards 88

C

cancellation charges/scale 25, 59
car parking facilities 25, 29, 63, 83
carpeting 30, 31, 48
cash, storage of 54
cash contribution 38
cash floats 54
CD-ROMs 24
ceremonies 90
checklists 67–9, 98
childcare 49
choice, importance of 38
cleaning services 80
cold 52
comfort breaks 64
communications 25
    on-the-day 66–7
community groups 17
community, sense of 85
computer screens 45–6
conferences 77–9

Organising Effective Events

confidentiality 93
contact details 61
contractors 80
convenience/availability of venue 93
co-ordination of delegates 79
correspondence 40–1
costs 26, 55
Council for the Advancement of Communication with Deaf People 34–5
customer satisfaction 74

D

databases 15, 17
date 7–10, 24, 25, 68
day of event 9
Deaf Community 34
delegate materials 37
delegate notes 51
delegate numbers 61
delegation 14, 98
demonstrations 90–2
departure time 25
dietary requirements, special 25, 56–7
dinners 50, 56, 74–7
disabled people 22, 64
  see also equality of access
discount arrangements 54, 58
displays 72, 80–2
documentation 40–1
down-the-line interviews 92, 94–5
drinks 75
  reception 56
drop-out rate 59
dryness 53

E

early booking incentives 58
editorial 18, 81
education 4
electrical items 80
emergency procedures 34
enquiries 14
entertainment 4, 76

entrance 30
equal opportunities 98
equality of access 27–38
  car parking 29
  entrance and registration area 30
  event rooms 31–2
  information and choice, importance of 38
  learning difficulties 37
  lifts 30–1
  mental health problems, survivors of 37–8
  microphones 28
  moving around venue 30
  overnight stays 32–3
  personal assistance 27
  physical accessibility 29
  refreshments 32
  sensory considerations 28–9
  sensory impairments 34–7
  staging 28
  toilets 31
equipment, booking of 97–8
evaluation 51, 70, 96
event literature 51
event plan 4–21
  aims and objectives 4–5
  branding and themes 10–13
  date 7
  format design 7
  marketing and promotion 16–20
  on-the-day staffing 20–1
  response mechanisms 14–15
  responsibilities/lines of command 13–14
  target audience 5–6
  timetables 20
event rooms 31–2
exhibition boards 47–8
exhibition space 80
exhibitions 31, 47, 80–2
exhibitors 61
extras 88

F

fairs 11, 82–3
feedback 70
festivals 11, 84–5
fêtes 11, 82–3
finding a venue 24
fire alarms 34
first aid 64
flipcharts 26
floorplans 62, 88
flowers 80
flyers 81
food *see* meals; refreshments
format 68
freepost address 58
fun fundraising 86
funding, mixed 39–40
fundraising special events 85–6
further information 59

G

geographical location 6
getting people to event 57–9
  agreement to attend 58
  turning up 59
give-aways 81
group bookings 58
guest list 87
guide dogs 36–7

H

handouts 51
health and safety 34, 83, 86, 92
hearing aids 35–6
hearing dogs 36
hearing impairment 28
heating 53
Hicks, Brian 27, 32, 33, 38
housekeeping 95
house-style for printed materials 10

I

"ice cream" stands 81
inclusiveness of participants 84
induction loops 28, 35–6, 44
information 38
  sharing 4
insurance 42, 54
interested parties 89
internal layout of venue 23
  see also floorplan
interpreters 28
  see also sign language interpreter
interviews, down-the-line 92, 94–5
invitations, written 58

J

joining instructions 41
Jones, Ruth 1, 7–8, 14, 16, 43, 58, 67
jumble sales 11

L

languages 51
large print 51
launches 89–90
leaflets 91
learning difficulties 37, 51
learning from others 21–2
legislation/legal issues 41–2, 86, 91
lifts 30–1
lighting 35, 47, 80
local businesses, involvement of 83
local press *see* media
location 23, 83
  see also geographical location
lunches 55–6, 58

M

Macpherson, Charlotte 2, 13, 59
  mailings 16–17
manufacture of prizes/merchandise 54

marketing and promotion 12, 16–20
  advertising 18–19
  editorial 18
  mailings 16–17
    posters 17
    telephone marketing 19
    word of mouth 20
materials 12
meals 72
  breakfasts 50, 55
  buffets 32
  dinners 50, 56, 74–7
  lunches 55–6, 58
media coverage 58, 59, 81, 89, 93–5
  see also photo opportunities; radio
mental health problems, survivors of 37–8
menus 75
merchandise 54–5
message boards 67
microphones 28, 43–4
mixed funding 39–40
monitoring mechanism 96
month of event 8
motivation 4, 82
moving around venue 30
music/sound effects 44, 81
Mussenden, Barry 5, 6, 8, 17, 44, 55–6

N

name/title of event 10
National Council for Voluntary Organisations 2, 13, 59
networking 22, 23, 34, 59, 65, 77, 85, 88, 95
newspapers *see* media
noise 53
no-refunds policy 59
notetakers 36
novelties 83
numbers and potential numbers of participants 6

O

on-the-day briefings 67
on-the-day communications 66–7
on-the-day staffing 20–1
open days 87–8
openings 89–90
organisation 6
outcomes 5
overhead projectors 26, 44–5
overnight accommodation arrangements 26, 32–3, 50

P

P/A system 43–4
pair work 32
participation 96
People First 37
performers 51
personal assistants 27, 31, 36
personal recommendations 24
petty cash 48–9
photo opportunities 90, 91, 92–5
physical accessibility 29
placards 91–2
planning 2–3
point-of-sale promotional material 54
post conference reports 79
posters 17
powerpoints 83
preparation 2–3
presentations 72
press conferences 92–5
price/delegate fee 23–4
prices 51
pricing display 54
pricing of auctions 73–4
pricing policies 5
primary audience 5–6
print 68–9
printed materials 10, 12
privacy 82
prize draws 88
prizes 54–5, 81, 83
profile, raised of organisation 85
programming 78, 84

Index

projectors *see* overhead; slide
promotions 5, 12, 54, 69
  see also marketing and promotion
protests 90–2
public areas, shared 25
publicity 5, 81, 90
purchase orders 41

Q

question times 79
questionnaires 70, 88

R

RAD 35
radio 18, 81
raffles/draws 83
rain 52
receipts 54
Red Cross 92
refreshments 26, 32, 55–6, 69, 80
  area and arrangements 23
  times 34
registration 26, 65
  area 23, 30
reminders 59, 60
reply-paid envelope 58
reporting mechanism 96
research 22
response mechanisms 14–15, 69
responsibilities/lines of command 13–14
reward 4
RNID 35
roadshows 80–2
room service 50
rooms 23, 25, 26
runners 67
running water, hot and cold 83

S

St John Ambluance 64, 92
sandwich boards 81

scheduling 78
season of event 8
seating plan 56
secondary audience 5–6
security 54, 80, 86
seminars 95–6
sensory considerations 28–9
sensory impairments 34–7
set *see* audio visual and set
setting up time 25
"shell schemes" 80
Sia 5, 6, 8, 17, 44, 56, 57
sign language 36
  interpreter 28
signposting 25, 51, 61–3, 88
slide projector 45–6
smoking 76
snow 52
sound-proofing 93
speakers 51
  scheduling and briefing 78
special diets 32, 56–7, 60
specialist booking agency 50
speeches 90
  length 95
spin-offs 85
sponsorship 5, 38–40, 70, 83, 85
  cash contribution 38
  mixed funding 39–40
  underwriting 39
staffing, on-the-day 20–1
staff/users, consultation with 87
staging 28, 47–8
status 6
stock control 54
sub-contractors 61
substitutes 59
sunshine 53

T

table plans 76–7
tannoy system 67
  see also P/A system
tape 51
target audience 5–6, 9, 16, 17, 51, 58
team 69

telephone marketing 19
telephones 67
temperature 53
themed events 10–13, 73, 74–7
things in writing 85
time of day of event 9–10
timetables 6, 20, 67
timing 51, 93
toilet facilities/cloakrooms 23, 26, 31, 51, 52, 63–4, 80, 83
tone of the event 5
tourist information offices 24, 25, 50
trade, increased for surrounding businesses 85
training 4
  days 95–6
transport/travel 23, 36, 50–1
turning up 59
type of venue 22–4

U

underwriting 39

V

venue 12, 68
  choice 93

layout 36
location 24
management 26
plan 51
staff 26
type 22–4
unusual 25
video equipment 46
vigils 90–2
visitors, co-ordination of 88
visual aids 29
visual impairments 29, 36

W

walkie talkies 67
water, jugs of 53
weather 52–3
week of event 9
word of mouth 20
workshop leaders 51
workshops 35, 95–6
workshop/syndicate groups 32

Y

year of event 8
Yellow Pages 17